P9-CND-132

# Everyday Grace

ALSO BY MARIANNE WILLIAMSON

*A Return to Love*

*Illuminated Prayers*

*A Woman's Worth*

*Illuminata*

*Enchanted Love*

*Emma and Mommy Talk to God*

*Healing the Soul of America*

R I V E R H E A D   B O O K S

*a member of Penguin Putnam Inc.*

*New York*

*2002*

# Everyday Grace

*Having Hope, Finding Forgiveness,*
*and Making Miracles*

Marianne Williamson

RIVERHEAD BOOKS
a member of
Penguin Putnam Inc.
375 Hudson Street
New York, NY 10014

Copyright © 2002 by Marianne Williamson

All rights reserved. This book, or parts thereof, may not
be reproduced in any form without permission.
Published simultaneously in Canada

Library of Congress Cataloging-in-Publication Data

Williamson, Marianne, date.
Everyday grace : having hope, finding forgiveness, and making miracles /
Marianne Williamson.
p.   cm.
ISBN 1-57322-230-5
1. Course in miracles.   2. Spiritual life.   I. Title.
BP605.C68W55      2002                    2002031757
299'.93—dc21

Printed in the United States of America

9   10   8

This book is printed on acid-free paper. ♾

BOOK DESIGN BY AMANDA DEWEY

*For Rich Cooper*

# Contents

# Acknowledgments

As I wrote this book, I was surrounded by three literary angels: Al Lowman, my literary agent for many years and once again my muse; Andrew Harvey, an extraordinary mystical author I am blessed to call my friend; and Wendy Carlton, the most dedicated editor I have ever known. All of them taught me not only how to make this a better book but, even more important, the true meaning of the word "support." If this book deserves any credit at all, then the credit belongs to them.

To Susan Petersen Kennedy, Riverhead's publisher, my thanks for both the inspiration and stalwart faith in my ability to deliver.

To Andrea Cagan, Alyse Martinelli, B. G. Dilworth, Charlette Manning, Matthew Albracht, Linda Puryear, Kathy Tomassi, Pam Rice, Suzannah Galland, and Christen Brown, with gratitude for help and encouragement.

To the many people who have supported my work at Renaissance Unity and throughout the world. I am surrounded in my dreams by your smiles and handshakes.

And to Emma, Mommy's darling. There really are no words.

A human being is a part of the whole called the "universe," a part limited in time and space. He experiences himself, his thoughts and feelings, as something separated from the rest, a kind of optical delusion of . . . consciousness. This delusion is a kind of prison for us, restricting us to our personal desires and to affection for a few persons nearest to us. Our task must be to free ourselves from this prison by widening our circle of compassion to embrace all living creatures and the whole of nature in all its beauty. Nobody is able to achieve this completely, but the striving for such achievement is in itself part of the liberation and a foundation for inner security.

ALBERT EINSTEIN

# Everyday Grace

# Introduction:
# Reclaiming Our Magic

My father used to speak of the Byzantine Rule, which is that nothing is as it appears to be. I have always had a sense that something is missing in this world—that at the very least there is something important we're not discussing.

I believe that hunger for a "lost dimension" of experience is a natural yearning in all of us, and it doesn't go away just because we ignore it. It is evidenced among other places in the millions of children and adults who obsessively read the Harry Potter books. It is said that fiction is where someone gets to tell the truth. We *are* a bunch of silly Muggles, and we really *do* miss out on the magic of existence. There's a collective knowing that a dimension of reality exists beyond the material plane, and that sense of knowing is causing a mystical resurgence on the planet today. It's not just children who are looking for a missing piece. It is a very mature outlook to question the nature of our reality.

We are like birds who have forgotten we have wings, kings and queens who have forgotten our royal heritage. We feel enslaved by conditions that should have no power to bind us, and powerless before forces over which we have been given dominion. No wonder our children are drawn to reading about a world in which people live a more magical existence than the one we offer them here.

I have watched my daughter bury herself, like so many other children, heart and soul in the Harry Potter books. I remember that when I was her age I had a similar fascination with books like *A Wrinkle in Time, Half Magic,* and the Narnia series by C. S. Lewis. In a particularly passionate moment, my daughter once told me that the only time she was really happy was when she was reading *Harry Potter.* And, sadly, I understood what she meant. It was the only place she felt she could stay in touch with all the magic.

When I am honest with myself, I know that I cry deep inside, just as my daughter does, when I cannot find the magic. Emma has asked me several times, "Mommy, are the Harry Potter books true? Are there really magical places like that?" And I answer her as honestly as I can, which is to say that I answer "yes." But she is never satisfied when I talk about different realms of consciousness, when I tell her that the magic in Harry Potter is a magic that lives in all of us. She wants a simpler magic, which I understand. And I assume that one day she'll find her own path to the magic that lives and breathes inside her. No one can take the journey for anyone else—even parents for our children—as much as we might like to. But if and when my daughter makes her own mystical journey, she will learn that magic indeed is here in this world right now. It is literally all around us. Each of us has a mark on our forehead, just like Harry Potter, that speaks to the fact that all of us come from a very magical source.

Harry Potter is one boy in a long line of mythical heroes who have reminded the human race that we are so much more than we think we are, so much more powerful than we seem to know. Jesus said that we would someday do even greater works than He; should we not take Him at His word? And should not "someday" be today? It's time for us to start working miracles, if indeed we have the capacity within us to do so.

This book is for those who seek to work miracles. The search for the Holy Grail of miraculous power—humanity's instinctive understanding that we are meant to soar above the limitations of our physical world—has been going on for ages. Yet now the search has become a popular yearning not just among monks or adventurers in far-off places, but among many of us living very practical lives. We wish to cultivate the sacred in the midst of the great and small difficulties of our daily existence. We want spiritual principles to be more than beautiful abstractions; we want them to actually transform our lives.

"Heaven and earth shall be as one," according to the Bible, meaning that one day we will live on the earth but think only the thoughts of heaven. The intersection between our material and spiritual existence is the mystical power represented visually in both the Christian Cross and the Jewish Star of David. It is the point where the axis of God meets the axis of humanity. The modern mystic is someone seeking to embody that point in his or her own experience.

In the words of author Manly P. Hall, mysticism is not a religion, but a "conviction of the heart." I realize now that the journey, which started in my childhood—beginning with books about magic, then moving on to philosophy classes, astrology, tarot, the *I Ching,* and ultimately more classical theological studies and *A Course in Miracles* (a self-study psychological training based on universal spiritual themes)—has been a fairly common version of my generation's spiritual journey. I was once someone—and in the

1960s and 1970s, there were many of us—who had moons and stars on the walls of every place I lived and encrusted in the jewelry of every outfit I wore. And we needn't discuss the Maxfield Parrish prints: the color, the light, the hint of another reality . . .

I can see now what I was going for, however crudely, and I have compassion for the young woman I was, always thinking there was "something more." Now that I'm firmly planted in my middle years, I can see that the spiritual path has been the calling of my soul for a very long time, and I am ready to devote the rest of my life to walking it as best I can.

The seeker in us is always seeking more Truth, knowing that the search goes on forever. The mystic in us, on the other hand, is trying to practice what we've learned of it: right here, in this moment, whatever we are doing. The mystic is a spiritual practitioner, seeking not merely to understand the principles of spiritual awareness, but to embody them as best he or she can. We embrace the idea—advanced by both ancient philosophers and modern physicists—that the world is one. Everything connects to everything; therefore, as we change, the world cannot but change with us.

Modern mystics form a kind of spiritual underground in the world today, seeking to transform *everything*. We are everywhere, as mystics have always been everywhere; we come from every religion, as mystics have always come from every religion; and some of us relate to no religion at all. The mystical realm lies beyond all dogma and beyond the evidence of the physical senses. The mystic has been called to an inner journey, through the darkened entanglements of human existence to the radical love at the heart of God.

I have written this book as a traveling companion for the modern mystic, who goes through his day with the deepest desire to be in the world but not of the world—to be walking with her feet planted firmly on the ground, but thinking with her head soaring powerfully through the sky. To live solidly grounded, but from a spiritual foundation, integrating within ourselves the consciousness of earth and the consciousness of heaven—such is the mystic's longing. And that longing is not for ourselves alone. For as any one of us finds our wings, the entire world is lifted.

The mystical path is not always easy, and my hope is that this book might be a bit of a map through some of its thorniest passages. I do not write as someone who has mastered the way, but as someone who has been walking it, though often clumsily, for several decades of my life. There are bits of information I've discovered on my way, pieces of knowledge and understanding that have made their way to me, as they've made their way to mystic travelers for generations. I have seen darkness, but I have glimpsed a little light as well.

May this book shed light on someone's path, and may all of us enter the illumined door beyond which darkness is no more. May the darkened skies of the human heart be lit by the Light of Truth. May the mercy and the peace of God be upon us now and for all our days.

Amen.

# PART I

# Thoughts of Grace

# The Mystical Wands

The first thing a mystic needs is his or her tools.

When I was a little girl, every August my mother would take me to the store to buy school supplies. First there was the important decision to be made about my lunch box. Did I want Cinderella on the front of it, or ballet shoes, or Snow White, perhaps? And then, of course, there were the notebooks, pencils and pens, erasers, and myriad other accoutrements, such as index cards, Marks-A-Lots, and notebook dividers. Only when I had all my supplies together was I prepared to go to school.

Ultimately I realized that tools are essential to almost any worthwhile endeavor. You don't go to school unprepared, you don't try to climb a mountain unprepared, and you don't walk the mystical path unprepared.

What are the mystic's supplies? They are spiritual principles, much like magical wands in their capacity to turn any situation into a crucible of miraculous transformation. They change the world by changing *us*. The mystic path is a journey of personal transformation, and while the goal of the journey is to become our true selves, we can only do this by letting go of who we are not. If we wish to experience the fullness of life, we must cut through layers of illusion that hide the truth of who we really are. The mystical path runs through a very deep forest—the forest of our own psyche—and we need our supplies in order to walk through it.

We meet monsters and demons on the inner path. We meet humiliation in order to grow to the point where our behavior would not lead to humiliation; we meet rejection in order to grow to the point where our behavior would not lead to the pain of rejection; we meet the pangs of deep regret in order to grow to the point where our behavior would not lead to regret. We meet the monsters in order to slay them. The only way to rid ourselves of darkness is by bringing it to light.

Until we have met the monsters in ourselves, we keep trying to slay them in the outer world. And we find that we cannot. For all darkness in the world stems from darkness in the heart. And it is there that we must do our work. The universe is holographic, which means the whole is present in every piece. Therefore, as we address the shadow within us, we *are* addressing the shadow of the world. The mystic does not deny the darkness, in ourselves *or* in the world, but affirms a light that lies beyond it. And we have faith the light will prevail because we have faith that light is our true identity. Our task is to remember that. We invoke the light by actively acknowledging it is there, standing as Harry Potter stood on platform 9¾, knowing the door would reveal itself because of the nature of who we truly are. Being magic, Harry lives in a magical world. And, being magic, so do we.

The mystical realm arises from a different mode of perception than the one we are used to. The human race now stands on the brink of a historic transformation, with new eyes, new ears, new minds, and new hearts emerging from the cosmic drama of human evolution. As an embryo becomes a baby, we are becoming a new, more spiritualized version of ourselves. We are growing mystical wings as we evolve, as any species does, in the direction that supports our survival. We are moving now toward a universal compassion because, if we do not, we will cause our own extinction. To be a mystic is to choose rebirth, for ourselves and for the human race. We are participating in a collective quantum leap forward, in which our species will experience a fundamentally new chapter in our history.

Fundamental change is not a casual occurrence. We cannot casually commit to the process of spiritual transformation. It's not enough to say, "Oh, I think I'll be a mystic this year." Mysticism is not a *trend*. Our entire being is called to the task, for the journey from density to light involves every aspect of who we are. Whether we are angry at the dry cleaners because they've ruined our favorite sweater, upset with a friend who has broken a promise, or frightened at the diagnosis of cancer in the breast of a best friend; whether we're worried about the state of our marriage, looking for a new job, or anxious about nuclear bombs and terrorists in our midst, we see that everything we go through is a step along the path. We are taking the mystical journey as a way of transforming the world by transforming *ourselves*. Only by finding the love within us can we provide the love that will save the world.

Each of us carries, in the depths of our consciousness, a boxful of mystical tools. And central to our tool kit is the magical wand. A wand is not just silliness from children's literature. Fairy tales are rife with archetypal truths that teach not only children, but open-minded adults as well, deep and fundamental truths about the nature of our reality. A wand is a medium of power, not just for wizards, but also for you and me. A wand is essentially a principle, an intention, a focused thought. When focused thought is negative, it creates ill. And when focused thought is loving and enlightened, it creates miraculous breakthroughs. A mystical wand is the illumined power that emanates from the mind when it is married to the heart.

Most of us love, to be sure. Yet far too often our love is passive; we must be proactive in our love in order for it to change our lives. Spiritual laziness has no place on the path. First, we must outgrow the myth of neutrality. For in fact there is no neutral thought; all thought leads to love or to its absence. One who is not committed to love is surrendered to that which opposes it, opening up the door to fear as surely as one who consciously welcomes that fear.

There is so much love in the human heart, yet hatred threatens our planet. And why? Because hatred is currently more committed than love. In the words of philosopher Edmund Burke, "The only thing necessary for evil to triumph is for enough good men to do nothing." Indeed, the forces of fear in this world are more disciplined, more courageous in a perverse kind of way, than are the forces of love. For hatred, as we know all too well, has no problem announcing itself and its intentions to the world. Our response should not just be that we *oppose hate;* our response must be that we *love the world.* Then and only then will love truly triumph:

when the children of God don't just *feel* our love, but *express* our love.

Our task then is to harness the energies of love—to actualize its enormous power in practical and meaningful ways. Love too must announce its intentions to the world, with all the passion born of a compassionate heart. We are a species that has everything, yet what we lack is what only we can give: conviction. It is the *conviction* to love that gives birth to miracles.

In the words of the French philosopher Teilhard de Chardin, "One day, after we have mastered the winds and the waves, gravity and the tides, we will harness for God the energies of love. And then, for the second time in human history, mankind will have discovered fire."

The mystic lives with that fire in our hearts. And that is why we use our wands, directing the power of their fiery glow to the darkened areas of human existence. Everything we encounter throughout the day is a spiritual opportunity, if we approach it with love. Every moment challenges us to rise to our highest: to choose strength over weakness, forgiveness over blame, faith over faithlessness, and love over fear. And when we can't, we ask God to help us. In choosing love, we are choosing to be healed from the forces that would hold us back. Love heals the world by healing our minds, for that which is healed on the level of consciousness is healed on the level of ultimate Cause.

The world will change when *we* change. We are living at a time when our technological power has so vastly outdistanced our spiritual progress that we are threatened by the prospect of global catastrophe. And yet there is within us the knowledge—etched on every human heart—that indeed there is a power beyond the mortal mind, which can do for us what we cannot do for ourselves. And if ever there was a time to humble ourselves, atoning for the arrogance of human conceit, it is now. There is a ripple of rising consciousness among the peoples of the earth today, as we consider the possibility that there might be a better way—a way the mechanical, rationalistic, technological left brain cannot access—which offers us hope that the mortal mind cannot.

There is another way of knowing, another way of living, and another way of loving on this earth. This "other way" is a realm that is full of magic and miracles. It is a world more real than what we see around us. It is the realm from which we have come, and to which all of us long to return. "As to me," wrote Walt Whitman, "I know of nothing else but miracles." Everything but miracles, in time, will dissolve in the presence of love.

Our imagination is the womb out of which a new world

will be born. Think of every situation in your life as being ripe for new birth. See luminous energy emerging from your heart, extending outward to touch all things. Cast the light over your childhood home. Cast it over your physical body. Cast it over warring nations. Cast it over the entire planet. Cast it over the people you love. Cast it over the people you judge. Feel now a bolt of energy coming over you as you extend this light. Avoid the temptation to invalidate this image. It's not an idle fantasy, for the light is real.

Now allow the light to flood your body, your blood, your bones. Allow it to illuminate your mind, your emotions, your relationships, your career. Congratulations. You have picked up your wand and begun to use it.

Our choice to stand within a field of infinite possibility is our miraculous authority in any situation. Changing our mental perspective is much like changing the lens on a camera. In the Bible it is written, "Be still and know I am." That moment of stillness is when our mental lens has a chance to refocus. And there, in a moment of sacred connection with all life, we know that only love is real. In the midst of war, we can quietly and powerfully know that peace is our natural state. In the midst of sickness, we can quietly and powerfully know that health is our natural state. To "know I am" is to know, and affirm, that only God's universe is real. Everything is a veil of illusion brought about by our illusion of separation from Him. Our greatest power to change our world lies in our power to see beyond the veil. For we will invoke the world we choose to see. This may mean we repudiate the testimony of our physical senses, or even of our logical minds. This repudiation is a positive denial of the so-called realities of a darkened world. As we stand firmly within a point of light—though darkness might be all around us—the darkness begins to dissolve into the nothingness from whence it came.

The attention we pay to the nature of our thinking, therefore, is the most powerful attention we can pay. Our spiritual victory lies in rising above the mental forces of fear and limitation, using our wands to purify our thought forms, thus attaining the power to heal and be healed. We will think anew and see anew. Such is humanity's next step: our spiritual challenge, our power, and our destiny.

# Miracles Happen

When I was a child, there was a well-known advertisement for V8 juice. Someone would drink something else and then realize, "Wow, I coulda had a V8!" As an adult, I've realized many times, when situations have not turned out so well, "Wow, I coulda had a miracle!"

I *could* have had a miracle . . . *except* . . . ! Except that I didn't think miracles were possible. I didn't think in a miraculous way. I didn't stand firmly on the principle that God can do anything. In the words of *A Course in Miracles,* "There is no order of difficulty in miracles." No problem is too hard for

God to solve. This is a very important point to remember, as it's hard to have deep faith in a kinda-sorta-powerful God.

Faith in God, however, is inseparable from faith in love. To say that there is nothing God cannot do is to say that there is nothing love cannot do. It does little good to ask God's help, if we ourselves remain unwilling to open our hearts in places where they are closed. It is not just God's love for us, but our love for each other, that paves the way for miracles.

If we fail to *express* God's love through faith or compassion or forgiveness, then the problem is not the absence of God's power but rather our failure to align our will with His. He cannot do for us what He cannot do through us. A house might be wired for electricity, but it still needs lamps if it's to be lit.

With every thought of miraculous possibility, the lamp is plugged in. A miracle is simply a shift in perception. The more we align ourselves with the principles of love, the more empowered we become. Children memorize the alphabet so they can learn how to read; we should memorize mystical principles so we can learn how to live most creatively. Each of us can live in the victory of spirit, claiming for ourselves the miraculous power that has been given to us as children of God. It is our *faith* that miracles are possible—that the very fabric of the universe is miraculous—which opens the mind, and thus the future, to unimaginable possibilities. "Dear God, please send a miracle" is a powerful prayer for cosmic support. To pray is to take spiritual action.

This earth is dominated by thoughts of fear, and we are conditioned by those thoughts to forget the power of our Source. Having not been taught the grandeur of our heritage, we do not remember the grandeur of our mission. We forget that we have the extraordinary power to work miracles in the name of God. Illusion and fear tie up the Prometheus inside us. No, we cannot do this or that, because we don't have enough money, or enough talent, or enough intelligence. No, we cannot change the world, because it's been the way it's been too long. No one needs to hold us down if we believe we're down already. As long as there are walls inside our minds, we're bound to remain behind them. For if you think you can't, you can't. If you think you can, you might. And if you think *God* can, you're on your way to a life of spiritual triumph. You have claimed His power on your own behalf, *which is what He would have you do.* God is not stingy with His miracles; it's a pity we ask for so few.

It's neither arrogant nor overreaching to ask for a miracle. Miracles aren't possible because of anything *we* do; they are possible because of the nature of God. We do not *personally* work them; rather, they are worked *through* us as we open our hearts more deeply to love. The mystical heart is a loving one, and thus a conduit through which God naturally reveals Himself. We have a power in us, but not of us, that can miraculously heal the entire world.

Perhaps the miracle arrives in the form of an insight that unlocks a riddle in your life, a reconciliation with someone, or the opening of a door that had long remained closed. Try as you might, your efforts to break through using your talents, your power of rational analysis, or sheer force of will had remained fruitless. It was only when you put God first—when your heart softened, you stopped blaming, you stopped talking so much and started to truly listen—that some wall of resistance began to crumble. You had not done anything so much as you had released the energies of self-will. You had asked, in a way, that God's will be done. A miracle occurred not because you caused it but because you allowed it. In the words of writer Willa Cather, "Where there is great love, there are always miracles."

Mystical consciousness is humble but self-confident. We are not relying on our own strength, but on God's. Science, technology, economics, military force, and social prestige—all of which are seen by the mortal mind as sources of genuine might and strength—might have the power to affect situations significantly. But they cannot work miracles. They cannot transcend the time-space continuum. They cannot transform the human heart.

Only love has the power to alter the subtler vibrations of human energy, for love transforms events on the level of consciousness, and consciousness is the level of true cause. The world outside us is a world of effects, so to merely change things within that world is to ultimately change nothing. Spiritual principle addresses the true cause of every problem, because every problem *is* in essence a spiritual crisis. Every problem reflects an unforgiveness. In every situation, the consciousness of love either has revealed itself or remains hidden. The role of the mystic is to find the love, and reveal the love, that lies latent in every circumstance.

Terrorism, for instance, is not our deepest problem, but rather the effect of a deeper one. Hatred itself is our deepest problem. While military power might contain the terrorists, only love has the power to dismantle the hate from which terrorism emerges. There is no problem to which the love of God—manifest in our love for each other—is not the ultimate solution. Yet we must look for that love within *ourselves*. A nation that puts money before love must address that problem first if we wish miracles to bless and protect us. It's not the *word* God, but the *work* of God, that is necessary in order to call forth miracles.

If miracles are seen as merely some sort of metaphor, then they are likely to have the power of metaphor in our daily lives. And how much power is that? Rather, we can see miracles as sewn into the fabric of the universe, and when we do, our experience of the universe is altered. When we are open to the possibility that God's power is truly unlimited—that in the ultimate vastness of the cosmos, love prevails—then we are automatically transported to a realm of possibility in which miracles flow forth naturally.

Why should we so slavishly surrender to a fear-based worldview that purports to have the answers to everything and yet clearly has answers to very few questions of fundamental import? The mortal mind can design a gorgeous wedding, but it cannot weave two hearts together; it can invent medicine to keep us alive, but it cannot create the will to live; and it can manufacture an engine of war, but it cannot create deep peace. Isn't it time to leave behind us the limitations of a mortal perspective and embrace instead the spiritual freedom that emanates from the Mind of God? Is not the world in some way upside down? Does the mortal mind deserve the adoration it receives, and the Mind of God such weak allegiance?

I've been in many circumstances where it simply didn't occur to me to ask for a miracle. I would think, *This situation isn't about God; it's about money, or work, or relationships, or politics.* But *any* situation is about God because He is the ultimate ground of our being. We are either standing on the ground of our true Reality, or we have forgotten who we are, throwing the universe off kilter and making ourselves vulnerable to the forces of chaos. According to the ancient Egyptians, the purpose of our lives is to preserve order in the cosmos. And we do this by preserving order within ourselves. Each one of us is—quite literally, according to modern science—the center of the universe.

Our relationship with God is our relationship with ourselves, for in no way are we separate from Him. Aligned with Him, we are firm within our own power; thinking ourselves separate from Him, we are cast into internal chaos and fear. To know that we are one with God is to know that we are infinite love. When we are not loving, we are literally not being ourselves. Infinite love is not an *attribute* of our being, but rather the *essence* of our being. Our only real problem is that we have forgotten who we are.

When we forget that we *are* love, we forget *to* love. And it is choice, not identity, that determines our experience. Should we wish to feel God's mercy, we must choose to be merciful. Should we wish to feel God's peace, we must extend God's peace. And should we wish to feel forgiven, then we must forgive.

It was not just the power of God, but the willingness of Moses to *receive* it, that caused the Red Sea to part. It was not just the grace of God, but the willingness of Jesus to *receive* it, that caused his resurrection. And it was not just the light of God, but the willingness of the Buddha to receive its illumination, that caused his enlightenment. It is in receiving God's love that we receive God's power.

When we want a miracle, we need simply to ask for one. In asking for a miracle, we are asking for a divine intercession, inviting the spirit of God to enter us and alter our perspective. It is useless to say, "Dear God, I want You to work a miracle, but I don't want to have to change my mind about anything." The Law of Cause and Effect is an immutable law of the universe. What we think is what we get, and God will not intervene between our thoughts and their effects.

When Cinderella's Fairy Godmother waved her wand— the Fairy Godmother representing the Divine Intercessor, as does Mary in Christianity, Kuan Yin in Hinduism, and Tara in Buddhism—a shimmering energy of golden light surrounded the object of her attention. We can think of this as transcendent energy brought to bear on any situation illumined by love. One attitude or perspective gives way to another, and the world is reborn. In the presence of the Fairy Godmother, mice turned into horses, a pumpkin turned into a carriage, and rags turned into a beautiful ball gown. Translated: People around us, *once we have shown more faith in them,* show up for us more powerfully than we had thought them capable; a job we had thought beneath us, *once we throw our creativity into it*, becomes the vehicle to a great success; our lack in some area, *once changed from a source of complaint to a source of thanksgiving for what we do have*, turns into a source of joy. *Any* situation can be redeemed. Overshadowed by the compassionate, faithful spirit of the divine, our lives become a space for miraculous new beginnings.

And new beginnings are possible anywhere, for there is nowhere God is not. Cinderella's Fairy Godmother worked with what was there: She didn't call a car service and order up a limo. She didn't call Saks Fifth Avenue and say "Bring me over something gorgeous." Rather, she surrounded what was already there with the illumination of divine under-standing, and what already existed then miraculously trans-formed. Miracles change the world, though not always externally. They may or may not produce results as the log-ical mind defines them, but they always produce at least sub-tle breakthroughs in the energies at the heart of a situation.

The word "discipline" comes from the same root as the word "disciple," and the mystic is a disciple of love. We are mentally disciplined to believe that there is no problem love cannot solve. Holiness is an internal state, a "whole" way of seeing. When our minds are no longer fragmented by the il-lusion of our separation from each other, but healed by the truth of our oneness, we are awakened to a new dimension of compassion. Within the mantle of that love, there is literally nothing we cannot do. We have remembered who God is. We have remembered who we are. Finally, we are whole at last.

# The Angels Are
# Waiting for *Us*

Every night before she goes to bed, my daughter says a prayer which I too said when I was her age: "Four corners round my bed, four angels round my head. One to watch, two to pray, and one to chase bad things away." It took me forty years to understand what a prayer like that is really saying.

Angels are the thoughts of God, and to ask for angels to gather near is to ask for God's thoughts to overshadow our own. To pray to an angel is to look to a level of pure thinking, divine thinking, and to ask that it replace our thoughts of fear. Such thoughts—of separation from others, as well as from God—are distortions of reality, mental "miscreations," and they lead us to conclusions and behavior that are destructive to ourselves and the world around us.

"One to watch": May the Spirit of love tend my thoughts, guarding the holiness that alone should remain on the altar of my mind.

"Two to pray": May I remain in conscious contact with God, ever alert to the miracles in my midst.

"One to chase bad things away": May God's Spirit cast out of my thoughts, and my world, the things that are not of love.

When we pray to something higher than ourselves, we are not praying to something outside ourselves. Angels do not live "somewhere else"—ultimately we realize that there *is* nowhere else—but simply in another realm of perception. They live within us as latent energies of divine power, potential but not yet actualized within most of humanity. In summoning angels, we're responding to the evolutionary lure of the angelic state. We're recognizing angels as spiritual mentors who can lift our thoughts to the heights of truth. And as we rise to meet them, we will ultimately become them.

With this second wand, we remember that it is our own responsibility, as best we can, to live up to the divine potential God has placed within each of us. We have our wings, should we choose to spread them. In almost any situation, if we're truly honest with ourselves, there are ways that we can fly higher, at fuller wingspan. There are ways to show greater honor and compassion to all life, to get over ourselves and serve something bigger. We are given as many opportunities to reconstruct the nature of our lives as there are moments in a day. We can think more insightfully, love more deeply, give more selflessly, and serve more faithfully the call of love. How many times have we regretted not having been kinder, or wiser, or more respectful to others? And how many times have we shown up lovingly for another person and been told, "Thank you. You're such an angel." Indeed.

Angel's wings are not just metaphorical, any more than a butterfly's are. Just because they don't materialize physically does not mean that they do not exist. They are an actual set of cosmic probabilities, increased in the presence of mystical awareness. They are higher thought forms through which we transcend limitations, flying above the earthly fears that would otherwise hold us down.

Humanity is now challenged as never before to actualize our divine potential, summoned by history to expand into the dimensions of mind and spirit that will divert us from a most destructive path. This is not a time to wait for angels, but to actively *become* them. Indeed, we are waiting for something that is waiting for us. The distance between

the lives we are living now and lives of mystical enchantment—between lives of material bondage and lives of spiritual freedom—is no farther than a decision to think
miraculously. Each time we consider a miracle impossible,
or assume that we ourselves are not capable of working it,
then we're choosing not to take flight. But that doesn't mean
that we can't, or that we won't. We will emerge from our
spiritual chrysalis into the light of a new state of being, when
human consciousness has realized our capacity to do so.

We need not wait for the world to become more mystical; the world *is* mystical. Our problem is not that the world
lacks magic; our problem is that we don't believe in its magic.
We do not show up fully for life, and then wonder why life
is not showing up more fully for us. I've seen so many people auditioning life, waiting for the *right* relationship, or the
*right* job, or the *right* house, before deciding to live life to its
fullest. People say, "When I've met the right person, I will
show up fully in a relationship. . . . When I have the right job,
I'll throw myself one hundred percent into it. . . . When I've
lost the weight, I will try to look great. . . ." Imagine a nar-
cissistic angel.

The time to show up fully for life is *right now,* whatever
the circumstances. The decision to *be* the divine attracts the
divine. Life is a swirling pool of infinite potential at every single moment, and we ourselves either activate or refuse to ac-

tivate the mystical fertility of the universe. The only way to achieve an exciting life is to be willing to be excited and exciting. The only way to achieve an excellent life is to be willing to be excellent. The only way to achieve love is to be willing to be more loving. Who and what we decide to be, in each and every moment, is reflected back to us in worldly forms. Situations that just "seem" to happen are not necessarily random at all. With every thought, we ourselves decide whether to welcome God's reality and its miraculous prospects.

As we convert our thinking—much as one converts an electrical current—from identifying with the material realm to identifying with the spirit, then our spiritual wings take flight. We are lifted above the limitations of the past, for when we approach a situation from merely a material orientation, we remain at the effects of material factors. But if we approach it from a spiritual orientation, we are freed from the confines of material factors. We are heir to the laws of whichever world we believe in.

Knowing this, the mystic says, "No, I am not buying into the notion that wealth and position determine my destiny. As a child of God, I am bound by nothing"; "No, I am not going to stop pursuing my dream because someone else doesn't see its value. As a child of God, I have the power to make dreams manifest"; "No, I am not wallowing in the victimization of a youth that did not go my way. As a child of God, I am able to transcend the past"; "No, I am not going to quiet my voice because other people are uncomfortable with my power. As a child of God, I am here to speak my truth."

The path to a transcendent sensibility is neither even nor easy at times, but the difficulty of the journey sometimes turns out to be its blessing. Indeed, there are ways in which the pain we suffered yesterday increases our power to work miracles today. For challenges teach us humility and faith. Having experienced the pain of a broken wing, and having been healed by the mysterious mercy of God, we then fly again with a distinctive grace.

No matter what suffering has marked our lives, if we are open to a miracle now, then a miracle can happen. And there is no greater miracle than a person becoming all that he or she can be. We are healed as we begin to realize that we will be who we decide to be. And it's never what we are not getting so much as what we are not giving that can actually hold us back.

I once knew a woman who wanted very much to become a partner at her law firm. She was being groomed for the position. Yet, as time went on, her hunger for partnership overshadowed her performance, as though waiting in the background was simply not her thing. She did not perform at her best. And by not living fully in the present, she actu-

ally doomed herself to the background, for she wasn't showing up more powerfully before she made partner, so no part-
ners in the firm could quite see how she had the stuff it takes
to ultimately join their ranks. She would have been better off
with a little less worldly ambition and a little more sense of
service.

When we choose not to be an angel, the angels in our
midst depart. People will tend to be to us what we have decided to be to them. Yet it can be difficult to shine on others when we do not honestly feel that there is light within
us. There *is* a light in all of us because God put it there. We
can look to those in the world who evolved to a higher level
of consciousness during their lifetimes. They were not made
of different stuff than we are so much as they made different decisions than we do. It was not *easy* for Abraham Lincoln to be the Abraham Lincoln we revere today; it was not
*easy* to be Susan B. Anthony, or Mahatma Gandhi, or Martin
Luther King, Jr. They were born, as all of us are, with potential greatness. But the actualization of that greatness was
not predetermined. They could have decided to do and be
otherwise. Whatever spiritual force moved within their
hearts, luring them toward a magnificent destiny, is a lure
that exists in all of us. There is no rational formula for greatness, for greatness is not rational. On some mysterious level,
despite whatever resistance they felt, the great are those who

simply said yes at times when others would have said no. Fear did not deter them so much as it honed them. Something called to them from a higher place, and they responded to what they heard.

Are we not being called by history to become the greatness that lies in us? What happens to this Earth now is up to us. We can remain who we are and sink further into the troubled world we have already made, or we can allow our hearts to crack open like cosmic eggs, out of which will emerge transformed creatures—our own true selves.

Look at it closely, in yourself and others, and tell me that creature does not have wings.

# Thoughts of Judgment
# Block the Light

When I was a little girl, anytime I would ask my mother something mundane—such as, "Are we going to go out to dinner tonight?" or "Are we meeting Daddy at the zoo?"—she would answer with a particular phrase: "God willing."

I never thought much of it when I was a child, but as I grew older it struck me how right she was. How often have people assumed this or that was going to happen, only to find themselves experiencing something very different indeed. You *think* you're going out to dinner tonight. But what's really true is that if something horrible like a car accident en route to the restaurant doesn't happen, *then* you're going out to dinner tonight. You *think* you're going to do this or that, but what you really mean is: If something out of my control doesn't interrupt my plans, then I'm going to do it. All of us are aware that God has to *agree* with our plans, or our plans will come to naught.

When my mother said "God willing," she was instinctively showing humility before the power of God. She knew it wasn't a good thing to assume that human will can totally control anything. And in saying "God willing," she was also praying that God *would* be willing—that God would bless our plans. I think she had all the bases covered.

In my parents' house, God was a given. I grew up to appreciate the meaning of the word "awe," as applied to the spirit of God. And that sense of awe has stayed with me all my life, only increasing as the years have passed. And I've moved from the realization that God is always present in my life to the realization that He is always *interested* in it as well. He's not a passive but an active force —and there is nowhere He is *not*. A God who created the world as one perceives it as one and loves it as one. That which *is* love cannot withhold love. His hand is in the tiniest details, whether they're a million miles away or right at the tip of my nose. His creation is a panoply of radiant genius reaching from the smallest wildflower to the mystery of quarks. The completely solid field of His presence, covering every aspect of existence, could not *not* include you and me.

Forget the idea that God has more important things to think about than you. This thought is not humble, but actually a thinly disguised arrogance. Could the Lord of the universe work at anything less than full capacity, surveying just some but not all of His creation? You will know that to God you are everything when He has become everything to you. God's infinite and imperturbable love is ever at work, creatively furthering the enhancement of good, everywhere and all the time. God has a plan for your life, and all life, which is perfect and unassailable. There is only one thing that can keep it from finding its way to your door, and that is you.

As children of God, we've been given free will: We can think with Him, or not think with Him. But we cannot limit the creative power of our thoughts. When our thoughts are thoughts of love, then we are aligned with and receive His power. When our thoughts are judgmental, then we are choosing to turn our backs to God. We can no longer see the light He is shining on us when we stop shining it on others.

Cinderella's Fairy Godmother did not say to Cinderella, "That stepmother of yours is such a bitch. . . . We'll show her!" She could not have said those things, or even thought them, and retained her mystical power.

"But," you might say, "the stepmother was so *mean* to

Cinderella, and the stepsisters were almost as awful! Doesn't the stepmother *deserve* to be judged?"

Notice that the Fairy Godmother obviously registered the fact that the stepmother was out of line, or she would not have stopped by in the first place. Clearly, she thought the situation needed to be rectified, or she wouldn't have brought her wand. But the Fairy Godmother was too wise to take sides. The archetypal wicked stepmother lives in all of us, as much as Cinderella does. The stepmother is not where we are bad; she is where we are wounded, divorced from our true nature. The Fairy Godmother came to heal, not to judge.

Cinderella's refusal to surrender to thoughts of retribution is part of what drew the Fairy Godmother to her in the first place. Hate can summon the powers of the world, but only love can summon the powers of God. It takes tremendous faith in the power of love to refuse to hate those who behave in hateful ways. Yet in that refusal lies our grace.

It can be very hard to love people who are not showing love to us. But God's love is a person's essential identity, regardless of how he or she acts. The miracle worker remembers a part of someone that they themselves have forgotten. People deserve love not because of what they do, but because of who they are. When someone has forgotten their love, they have fallen asleep to who they are; our mystical

challenge, and our spiritual power, lies in choosing to remain awake.

No one was ever born to hate. God's love in our hearts
cannot be destroyed but only temporarily put to sleep. We
must know this and refuse to forget it, about ourselves and
about one another. The perception of someone's innocence
is a choice we make, based not on our opinion of them, but
on our knowledge of God. The realm of personality, with all
its good and bad, is not the realm of spiritual Truth. It is
a "fallen" realm. And we can escape it through the act of
forgiveness.

While we can choose to remain focused on the realm of
personality, it is not a realm of miracles. Focus on guilt will
always breed fear, and focus on innocence will always breed
love. Any time we project guilt onto someone else, we are
fortifying the experience of guilt within ourselves. Like
blood on Lady Macbeth's hands, we cannot remove our own
guilty feelings as long as we are judging others.

Whenever you are angry, know you're hurting *yourself*.
Ask for a healing. Ask to experience your own angelic nature,
that you might see beyond someone else's behavior to the
angel, however wounded, within them. Given the unity of all
minds, what we do to others, and what we think about others, boomerangs back to us. If we wish to feel peace, then

we must wish peace for others. And whatever punishment we wish upon others, we subconsciously attract to ourselves.

Withholding judgment is a powerful wand, because often people show us what we invite them to show us: If I respond to your guilt, you will tend to show me more of it. If I approach you with a critical attitude, then I'm more likely to get a response from you that seems to prove my point. Yet if I respond to your innocence, you'll tend to show me that, as well. Our focus on the good in someone else, regardless of whether or not our ego thinks they "deserve" it, casts a mystical light on any relationship.

This principle holds true whether we speak judgmentally or even *think* judgmentally. Sometimes we feel that if we clean up our behavior ("If you can't say something nice about a person, then don't say anything at all!"), then that will be enough. But it is not. Our thoughts, not just our actions, create our experience. People telepathically register your real thoughts, regardless of whether you are consciously aware of them or not.

Also, we don't get points for having "little" judgments rather than "big" ones. Any diversion from love is a fundamental diversion from love. At the same time, we're human, of course. We are not asked to be perfect, but to be honest— to pray, "Dear God, I have judgments about this person, but

I am willing to see the situation differently. Please show me his innocence, so I will no longer focus on his guilt. Please make this a lesson in love and not fear. Amen."

There is a way to affirm the divine perfection in a person, even while responding to their human flaws. And when we do—when we choose to affirm someone's basic goodness even when needing to share constructive criticism or complaint—we open doors to communication that otherwise remain closed. From an employer to an employee, for example, "Excuse me, but this was not done correctly" is not a particularly miraculous communication. On the other hand, something more along the line of "I want you to know how valuable your work is, and how much of a contribution you are making here. Also, I would like to have you work on this particular project *this* way" is very different. It's a statement that affirms the heart and therefore opens the mind, providing the space for genuine communication untainted by resentment or fear.

If our goal is simply to "get something done," then we're often tempted by the delusion that our ego is the best guide to action; however, if we're interested in miracles, then we listen to the voice of Spirit, which would have us put the focus on a person's innocence before a focus on their guilt. This is sometimes easier said than done, but the ability to do so can make a tremendous difference.

When we realize our mission is to love and forgive, we realize that every situation is an opportunity to do so. What we might see as a problem is looked at differently when we recognize that every event is part of a divine curriculum, set up by God for our growth and healing. Sometimes our challenges in one area provide answers in another. A problem with a nasty neighbor becomes an opportunity to use our spiritual power, praying for someone as a way to resolve conflict. Dealing with a difficult employee becomes an opportunity to work on communicating compassionately, without compromising our truth. Having to make a difficult decision becomes an opportunity to surrender, learning how to ask God for guidance. Every situation is a lesson in becoming who we are capable of being.

Every situation is ultimately a lesson in forgiveness. Forgiveness is our decision to see the love that is real in all of us, despite whatever appearances to the contrary there are. Fear melts away when we refuse to affirm its ultimate reality. When we see *beyond* fear, it dissolves. I no longer blame you because I don't believe the part of you that acted out is who you really are. I relate instead to your innocence, to the angel within you, which remains, no matter what you do. That is the power of forgiveness: to call forth a higher reality by *acknowledging* a higher reality.

Think of the Israelis and the Palestinians. They are

locked in war, but that is not who they are. They are one in spirit, as we all are, beyond the mortal plane. We will not find peace in the world by *fixing* the mortal plane, but by *transcending* it. Knowing that warring peoples in fact are one—holding to this mystical truth despite appearances to the contrary—establishes a womb for the rebirth of their relationship. While they are having such an understandably difficult time seeing the love in each other, all of us can help by seeing it for them.

Because all minds are joined, deep peace cultivated anywhere is a blessing on people everywhere. What we do on the level of consciousness affects what happens in the realm of bodies, far more than what we do in the realm of bodies affects the level of consciousness. Einstein said we would not solve the problems of the world from the level of thinking we were at when we created them. Situations such as the Middle East conflict are examples of both our challenge and our opportunity to move our awareness to a higher level.

Forgiveness is our mystical function, but it's often a gradual and quite painful process. Forgiveness doesn't mean that we pretend to like whom we do not like, or turn a blind eye to the evils of the world. Commitment to God's love doesn't destroy our capacity for discernment. But the way of divine compassion—though not an easy path, though often counterintuitive—is the next step in humanity's evolutionary journey. It's the *only* step that will enable us to survive the storm of hatred raging around the world.

Judgment is like an eclipse of the sun, which blocks its light. Spiritual light, it has often been said, is like the light of a thousand suns. We come from the light, and will return to the light, when light is all we choose to see. We will know that we are home in God when we are home in one another's hearts.

God commanded us to love one another as a way of removing from our midst all that is not love. Jesus did *not* say, "Love each other, *but only under certain circumstances.*" His kingdom, He said, is not of this world. And neither is ours.

# The End Is Inherent
# in the Means

When Mahatma Gandhi articulated his principles of political nonviolence, he stressed that, in all our doings, the end is inherent in the means. This concept reverses the common Western truism that "the end *justifies* the means." According to Gandhi, *how* we do something is as important as *what* we're trying to do, because ultimately whatever we do will be *determined* by how we do it. Who we are as we go through a process—whether we choose integrity, faith, and compassion or their opposites—affects the outcome of a situation more powerfully than the mortal mind admits. Love is a process as well as a goal.

As we concentrate on being the people that God would have us be, a path of light opens up before us to ease our way. Circumstances begin to fall into more harmonious patterns as we find more harmony within ourselves. We can tell when a situation is in the "flow," when we're no longer paddling upstream, when there is less stress involved in making something happen. The effort to align ourselves with the holy and good is our greatest power to affect external situations.

So it is that if we foster good cause, then good effects will ensue—not always immediately, but *ultimately*. In the words of Martin Luther King, Jr., "The moral arc of the universe is long, but it bends toward justice." There are laws of the universe that do not change. If we take care to honor the roots of a tree, then the trunk and the branches will take care of themselves. The mystic surrenders to the flow of God's love, knowing that it flows naturally in the direction of the highest good for all. There is a spiritual *beneficence* at the center of the universe. And as we gain, through experience, more and more faith in that basic goodness, we learn to give up our efforts to control and instead begin to deeply trust. It is not human will or personality we are trusting, or human machinations of any kind; rather, we're placing our trust in the Law of Cause and Effect, or karma, which is God's blueprint for the spiritual workings of all creation.

The world is rife with human suffering. And yet there is,

behind the worldly veil of darkness and fear, another possibility, a truer reality than that which we are living now. Our capacity to reach beyond the veil does not emanate from what we do, but from whom we are audacious and devoted enough to now become. That is why entering deeply into the still waters of God's love is every bit as important as any external action we take if we are serious about trying to change the world.

Mental and emotional agitation are obstructions to the flow of God's love into the world, reflecting as they do our separation from the peace of God. In order for the world to heal, human beings must realign our hearts and minds with Him. For in that union of God and human—the esoteric meaning of the Christ mind—a wondrous cocreative power emerges, bringing with it a blessing on all the world. This power is a correction of all our mental miscreations, restoring harmony and order to every aspect of our lives. When our minds are healed, the world will be healed, and nothing that does not vibrate with love will long remain.

Love is literally the power of God alive on earth. It is a transformative, alchemical, miraculous *force*. And with that force, God is well aware of how to make this universe work perfectly for all of us. Yet often we do not allow it, however strongly we profess our belief in God's love as our salvation. For God's love is not just His love for us; it is, most important, the love we give the world. The highest commandment is that we love *one another*. And when we make the extension of that love our primary goal, no matter the circumstance, those circumstances are blessed.

We must take the actions that bring love to life, making it the organizing principle behind all our endeavors. Business should reflect it; politics should reflect it; education should reflect it; everything should reflect it. Love is more than sentiment, and writing in lights across the sky is not enough to bring it forth; we must sow its seeds in the ground beneath our feet. Sometimes we *intend* to love and yet remain unwilling to love.

Why do we consistently refuse to allow love to light our way? We resist the allure of love, while still longing for its comfort. And what is that resistance, really? First, it is resistance to the experience of a bigger life, in which our small and separate identity disappears. What is actually the birth of our spiritual identity feels to the ego like death. The ego, our small and separate sense of self, is an imposter personality. It is a false self. It resists our genuinely remembering God, because in the recognition of our oneness with Him lies the death of the ego and the end of all fear.

Second, we resist love because it jams the rational mindset. The mortal mind cannot understand how miracles work, and for our entire lives we are taught to mistrust what cannot be rationally explained. Yet the fact that we cannot understand how miracles work does not mean that miracles don't happen. And while Western science argued for ages that the state of our inner being has little effect on the state of our world, even science today argues otherwise. Heisenberg's Uncertainty Principle reveals that as our perception of an object changes, the object itself will change. The relationship between our internal and external realities involves a quantum phenomenon inaccessible to the mind, yet accessible to the heart.

We can safely place our lives in the hands of God, as His Spirit knows far better than we do how to turn our earthly existence into streams of radiance. Yet the ego stands guard, lest we break free of our self-destructive patterns. The ego, after all, cannot live without them.

Think of the woman who is so intent on getting her boyfriend to marry her that she can't simply love him without an agenda. She feels the need to control the relationship in a way that's not possible if her only goal is the peace of God for her boyfriend and herself. Her neediness, of course, does not bring her love, but in fact repels it.

And think of the committed political activist who is so intent on fighting a wrong that he or she fails to honor the basic humanity of the opponent. Time and time again, the anger that feeds our political passions can be the very thing that invalidates us in the eyes of those we most wish to persuade.

The woman would best realize that the future of her relationship depends on the state of her being as she relates to her boyfriend now. The activist would best realize that there is no creating a loving world except through our willingness to *be* the love we wish to see. Sometimes it's less important to know how the world works than to know how *change* works. We cannot change anything unless we ourselves are willing to change, for whatever problem we see in the world is only there as a reflection of our own internal state.

We beat the Nazis, but the world is not yet rid of evil. We outlawed slavery, but our nation is not yet rid of racial tension. World War II could not end hatred, and the Emancipation Proclamation could not end racism. The deeper changes we are seeking to effect, in ourselves and in the world, are dependent on a level of inner transformation that no external force can dictate. Former generations did their part, and now we must do ours. We must work assiduously on the process of self-purification, for whatever we do to improve the world will be infused with the energy with which we do it.

We cannot *give* what we do not *have:* We cannot bring peace to the world if we ourselves are not peaceful. We cannot bring love to the world if we ourselves are not loving.

Our true gift to ourselves and others lies not in what we have but in who we are.

I have noticed how different I am, depending on the way I begin my day. In the first scenario, my daughter goes to school, and I sit down with a good cup of coffee and *The New York Times.* I enjoy the coffee, the paper, and the morning time by myself. When I'm finished reading, I check my e-mail, dress, and go to work. This is fairly enjoyable and fairly productive. But I realize it's guaranteed to maintain the status quo in myself and those around me.

In the second scenario, I carve out at least twenty to thirty minutes each morning to spend quality time with God. It takes a little more self-discipline but offers an immeasurably greater gift to my life. For during this time, my mind is freed of mental patterns that would keep me tied to yesterday. I light a prayer candle and pray out loud, sharing with God my hopes and fears that day. I seek to atone for my own mistakes, and I seek to forgive others for theirs. Then I meditate silently, entering the deeper waters of the divine. I am a student of *A Course in Miracles,* as well as a Transcendental Meditator, but I don't think it matters what form our spiritual practice takes. What's very important to realize, however, is that the mind of someone who regularly practices prayer and meditation *is literally a different mind.* I know this is true of myself, simply from my own experience.

In what ways am I different? Certainly I am more serene, which affects all my interactions as I move through the day. Also, I think I'm *smarter*. I have greater insight, I view situations with greater depth, and my mind is not so cluttered with the meaningless preoccupations that bombard us each moment in this increasingly frantic world. My spiritual practice doesn't just make me *feel* better; I think it makes me a different woman than I am when I choose not to do it. Everything I'm involved with becomes infused with a peace I do not otherwise carry. It affects the reactions of people I meet and the outcome of situations I might not even know exist.

We don't need to push life so much as we need to experience it more elegantly, to be motivated more by inspiration than by ambition. Sometimes we're so intent on moving up the ladder that we make compromises we know we shouldn't make while we're on the lower rungs. Yet faith is a ladder that leads to new heights. We are here to do what God would have us do; our prayer is to receive guidance not only as to what that is, but also how to do it in any situation. We can remain in the realm of divine understanding, for our depth of understanding *is* the key to the life we truly want.

When process matters most, we find that the deeper life is a mysterious river, leading us to places we would otherwise fail to go. The mortal mind says, "I'm going to Boston for the week, to work on a new project." The mystic realizes that every point in our journey is part of a mysterious unfolding. We would pray, "Dear God, I surrender my trip to Boston and ask that it be used on Your behalf. I go to Boston in the service of the Light, that the love in my heart might be of use to someone. I am open to all the miraculous possibilities that could arise from this trip. I bless in advance everyone I will meet there. My goal is to experience the spirit of God in everyone I see, that I might receive the gifts that are in store for me. May I be, do, and say according to Your Will. Amen." Just saying such a prayer automatically places us in a blessed space, and a greater life follows.

The normal business trip mentality might produce financial gain or a promotion, but it won't necessarily produce joy. The mystic's attitude is open to an abundance that is not of this world. And from that internal abundance flows good that the mortal mind can scarcely imagine, and not just for ourselves or for one particular circumstance. Any gift that is given by God is a gift that is meant for all of us. There is no end to the miraculous effects extending into the world when our minds are one with Him. Every prayer from the heart— be it for our career, or our family, or our nation—is a prayer for the world, whether we know it at the time or not.

"Dear God, please make me an instrument of your peace. . . ." is one of the most famous lines of prayer. And there is good reason for that. We know it speaks to something profoundly practical and real that will, if we allow it to, overcome all the darkness and hatred in the world.

"Dear God, please make me whom you want me to be, and take me where you want me to go." Such is the surrendered prayer of one who has figured it out, that all roads that lead away from God are roads that take us nowhere.

# Sacred Silence
# Rights the Universe

In fairy tales like *Snow White* and *Sleeping Beauty,* an innocent maiden is walking through the woods with all the animals of the kingdom gathered around her, in harmony with one another and with her. Birds flock around her, as though to guide her, should she lose her way.

That image—of the sleeping beauty that lies within us all, snow white in its innocence and purity of spirit—is a subconscious message to children and adults as well, that when we're aligned with our own spiritual essence, the world is a safer place to be. Remaining serene within ourselves, we become magnets for harmony and peace in the world.

Yet the world is hardly ever a peaceful place, and you and I are not Sleeping Beauty. Inner peace is a real prize in these times; in the words of John Lennon, "I'd give you everything I've got, for a little peace of mind." As difficult as it can be to find genuine inner calm, it is the key to creating peace in the world as we know it. The world will not change until we do, and there is nothing the world can deliver to us that will give us the peace we crave. Peace comes not from the world, but from God.

In any given moment when the world is too much with us, we can take a deep breath and travel home to the inner room inside our minds. There sits God on His radiant throne, always there to receive us in the sanctuary of the heart. He never abandons us, though we abandon Him so frequently. It is built into the design of creation that the Prodigal Son—whether we've been gone for ten minutes or ten years—can always return home, in any moment we choose.

The door to God swings open at the slightest knock. The portal that takes us from the hysteria of a fear-based world to the peace and love of God is any moment of pure and sacred silence. It only takes one moment, perhaps one good deep breath, in which we inhale the love of God and exhale the madness of the world. We wait in silence to receive His Spirit, willing to soften our heart, no matter how much we need His help to do so. It is a moment when we're willing to forgive anyone and everyone. And it is a moment when we're willing to pray for a miracle, asking for a ray of light to break through whatever darkness is surrounding us at that moment.

I once saw a pseudo-Buddhist graffito that read, "Don't just do something—*sit* there!" It's humorous, but it's also a good spiritual directive. Where the ego would have us believe, "I've got to do something! I've got to do something!" the spirit would have us remember, "The best thing I could do would be to sit down and quietly seek the peace of God."

The Western mind, particularly, is bent on the notion that we must do something all the time. However, when we remember that consciousness precedes matter, we recognize that serenity is more than a beautiful feeling. It's an essential strength. An agitated mind creates an agitated world, which then creates more agitated minds, which then create a more agitated world. But moments of sacred silence break the vicious cycle. And that is why the cultivation of such moments is one of our wands. It harmonizes everything.

Advertisements constantly hawk the latest pharmaceutical answers to our lack of inner peace. Yet all of us know, deep within, that psychic pain, like physical pain, is there for a reason. We don't heal a broken leg by numbing it, and we don't heal a broken heart that way, either. Ultimately, only the alchemical processes of spirit can actually disentangle the thought forms that cause our distress, guiding us to forgive one another and reconnect to God. When we're overshadowed by the Spirit of God, it's as though He's performing psychic surgery on our souls. We are literally transformed in heart and mind, as His peace comes upon us. It doesn't come in pill form, but it comes.

A moment of sacred silence is our cosmic reset button. My niece Meredith is a third-grade teacher, and she puts a moment of silence to great use when her students are beginning to spin out of control. "Stop!" she says, putting a palm out in front of her like the Supremes singing, "Stop, in the name of love!" Then she says, "Take a deep breath," and inhales. Then she taps the fingers of one hand to the side of her head, counting out loud to five. Then she slowly exhales. The kids inhale and exhale right along with her.

The first time I saw her do this, I thought, *Wow. I wish someone had taught me that when I was in the third grade. My whole life would be different!* I've remembered that technique, and I've used it a few times myself.

There are clearly times when quieting down and bringing our energy back into ourselves is a step toward inner peace. Yet the most powerful life is not one in which we bring ourselves back to our center when we have spun away from it, but rather one in which we seek to live from that center at all times.

One day I was sitting with my little girl on a bench in a public square, watching some college students play Frisbee in a field across the street. We were with several friends, chatting and making plans for the afternoon.

"You know, darling," I said to my daughter, "it seems, from a worldly perspective, that the people who are running around on that field are the ones who are moving energy, making things happen. And you and I sitting on this bench talking are not really doing anything.

"But, from a metaphysical perspective, you and I are moving energy, too. If you can really sit still at a moment like this, with your spine erect, deeply breathing in and out, and feeling love in your heart for everyone, then you're actually moving more energy around than someone who's playing Frisbee. When you learn to be really still, surrendering your mind to God, you are learning to summon energy from the furthest reaches of the universe. Your mind becomes like a magnet attracting the most positive things.

"The more still you become, the more the universe moves into powerful action on your behalf. Forces you will never be consciously aware of begin to move in your direction. The less still you are—the more emotionally and mentally fidgety you are—the more the universe stays stuck in old patterns of energy, reflecting the general chaos of your own psyche."

As I relished the thought of my daughter as my spiritual apprentice, I also realized she was merely tolerating my metaphysical musings. But I continued, "And that is because the tenor of your being, not your doing, is what establishes the pathways of energy that run through your life experience. Those pathways are real, and not just symbolic. They are the trains of thought, firing of mental synapses, and subconscious instincts to act and react that lie within each of us. Our goal is to purify that mental and emotional energy, so that the pathways of potentiality surrounding us are full of only love and creativity. It is fearful and destructive thoughts that set up fearful and destructive patterns in our lives.

"Okay? Do you get that?" I asked, hugging my daughter's shoulders close to me.

"Sure, Mom," she answered sweetly, patting my hands as though she wanted to reassure me she'd be there to comfort me when they arrived to take me away. We both laughed. But I figured then, as I do now, that if I throw out seeds, who knows? We often hear things that make no sense when we hear them and then blossom in our consciousness years later.

I was no different when I was young. In my twenties, I read a lot of literature by Indian gurus. Their spiritual wisdom often went way above my head, and it seemed they would respond to just about any query with the same advice: "Meditate." In those days, I had little patience for such simplicity. *Who are these people, anyway?* I thought. *What do they know? They don't even date!*

But I hear that advice much differently now. I've realized that no matter what the problem, the single most powerful thing I can do is be quiet—go to the place of holiness in my own heart, release my attachments and unforgiveness, and surrender myself to God.

I've thought about what would happen if we were to be able, for one twenty-four-hour period, to get every single person on earth to remain totally quiet. And I believe that, were we able to do it, we would at the end of that one day have fundamentally altered the collective consciousness, and thus the destiny, of the human race. When enough of us learn how to become deeply, profoundly quiet, then the hysteria of the world will begin to subside.

Following my lectures, I usually hold a question-and-answer period. And I know from experience how different the questions are, both in quantity and in substance, depending on whether or not we meditate before the questions begin. That's because many of the questions we carry around with us have less to do with genuine issues, and more to do with the monkey mind itself. A trickling flow of hysteria pervades our day-to-day mental functioning, constantly influencing our thoughts and emotions. This subtle hysteria is our biggest problem, because it's the root of all others. When our minds are aligned with God's love and peace, two things are true. First, we don't create as many problems in our lives. And second, we have the spiritual strength to handle them powerfully and positively when we do.

Genuine quiet, however, is far more than a behavioral condition. I have seen "quiet" people who were clearly seething with rage. Mystical quiet is achieved through the radical purification of prayer and meditation, combined with the consistent effort to love and forgive. You can be having a deep massage on the most beautiful beach in the world, on the most beautiful day of the year, but if you're harboring judgment and resentment, then your mind is still agitated and you will not know peace. Our world is full of noise and violence, and it takes more than a house in a quiet neighborhood to achieve a quiet mind. Whatever our meditation technique, what is important is that we meditate. Whatever or whomever we need to forgive, what's important is that we forgive. And whatever life presents us with in any given moment, what is most important is that we live in the temple of God. Our mind is His altar, and our heart is His sanctuary. The outside world is a realm of illusion, and its gifts, if we are attached to them, become the gifts of pain.

Staying within ourselves, feeling the center of our own

being, we allow the power of God to give us everything we need. Living there, we can always work miracles. Living outside, we will always be in need of them.

As we release our need to be "seen," to be clever, to achieve, or to perform, the way is made clear for our inner radiance to shine. In a noisy world, seek the silence in your heart. And through the power of silence, the energies of chaos will be brought back to harmony—not by you, but through you, as all miracles are.

When we visit that silence regularly, particularly in the morning, then the days of our lives become lit from above. Darkness and fear are cast from our midst, slowly at first, one moment at a time. Ultimately, all darkness will be gone from every heart. A deeper peace within your heart brings peace, in time, to everyone—for in truth, the world is one. Mystics are a spiritual underground providing the spiritual medicine that will heal the human race.

We have our wands now. We're prepared to begin.

# Abracadabra

Spiritual mastery lies not just in understanding the wands, but in using them. It's like the difference between Cinderella's Fairy Godmother explaining how the light works and her actually taking out her wand and waving it around a few times. One describes the transformation of a pumpkin into a coach, while the other actually makes it happen. It's time for us to take out our own wands now and transform a few pumpkins of our own.

"Abracadabra and fiddle-dee-dee, my ego is outraged to see the new me. . . . Abracadabra and hody-ho-ho, my former neuroses, where did they go?"

Every day we're confronted with a gap, often painfully wide, between the life we live now and a life of deep enchantment. As much as we might want to believe in the power of spiritual principles, we often feel like we don't know how to apply them. At times, they seem so far away from our practical realities. Yet, in fact, they are only as far away as our next perception, should that perception be filled with love. No matter what the circumstance, we can choose to infuse it with light.

In every hour of every day, dealing with small details or dealing with huge issues, the alchemical power of our spiritual wands provides a portal into another realm, a magic carpet ride above the turmoil of the world. This is not illusion, this is reality. From the time we awake to the time we go to sleep, heaven's light—the understanding of higher principles—is available to us, should we have the courage to bring it down.

We will not find true light in this world, for the thought forms that prevail here are guilt-ridden and fear-based. We will only find light in God, who gives it to us that we might extend it to every living thing. Every moment of every day, becoming more illumined, we become the illuminators. Eventually darkness shall be no more.

Yet miracle-working is not a part-time job: We must bring to the table everything we are and all our experience.

*Miracles happen.* It's one thing to know that, but another to apply it. *The angels are waiting for* us. It's one thing to know that, but another to apply it. *Thoughts of judgment block the light.* It's one thing to know that, but another to apply it. *The end is inherent in the means.* It's one thing to know that, but another to apply it. *Sacred silence rights the universe.* It's one thing to know that, but another to apply it.

And yet apply these principles we must, if we are to be serious agents of the sacred. And that is what comes next: bringing wisdom and grace from the abstract realm to the practical realm, where cars get rusty and our bodies grow old, where the news is so bad at times and life so sad. Hour by hour, day by day, we can find more light within ourselves, and the world will begin to shine.

# PART II

# A Day of Grace

8:00 am

# Starting the Day

*It's the beginning of your day.*
*You awake and look around you,*
*feeling perhaps a joyful expectation,*
*or perhaps an awful dread.*
*No matter which, remember this:*
*God loves you with an infinite love. . . .*

At the beginning of the day, the mind is most open to receive new impressions. One of the most important things we can do is to take full responsibility for the power of the morning.

If you want to have a *non*miraculous day, I suggest that newspaper and caffeine form the crux of your morning regimen. Listen to the morning news while you're in the shower, read the headlines as you are walking out the door, make sure you're keeping tabs on everything: the wars, the economy, the gossip, the natural disasters . . . But if you want the day ahead to be full of miracles, then spend some time each morning with God.

Most of us wouldn't think of beginning our day without washing the accumulated dirt from the day before off our bodies. Yet far too often we go out into the day without similarly cleansing our minds. And our minds carry more pollution than our bodies, for they carry not only our own toxicity but that of the entire world. We carry the fear, anxiety, stress, and pain not just of our own lives, but of our families, our nation, and millions all over the planet.

Our greatest weakness is the weakness of an undisciplined mind. We need not let fear steal the morning; we can consciously choose not to allow our minds to be programmed by the worldly viewpoint that dominates the earth. We can set our day upon another course. Each of us has an inner room where we can visit to be cleansed of fear-based thoughts and feelings. This room, the holy of holies, is a sanctuary of spiritual light. The light is not a metaphor, but rather an actual energy of mystical vibration. When we begin our morning within it, the mind receives a radiance that illumines our thinking as we go through our day.

Imagine yourself sitting in a perfect, comfortable spot for meditation. It might be a chair in your bedroom or living room. It is a place of relative quiet and calm, where you go on a regular basis to find the peace that only God can give.

You have come to realize that this time of rest, in its stillness and peace, is beneficent to both your mind and body. Here you come to surrender to God, using a prayer or mantra to move beyond the frantic and overwhelming thoughts that stalk us night and day. You are making your daily pilgrimage home, where your life will be renewed.

While the power of such quiet time can be profoundly healing, we often resist it fiercely. We have scores of reasons why we don't have time to meditate: "The kids have to get off to school. . . . I have to go to work. . . . My partner wants to be with me. . . . I have early appointments . . . ," and the list goes on. Yet none of those excuses would be used to avoid taking a shower or getting dressed. It would be ludicrous to say, "I'm just too busy. I had to give up showers." And yet "busy-ness" is a common excuse for why we do not take the time, or give the time, to meet regularly with God.

Just think about it: We turn down the chance for a meeting with *God*. It's a meeting He is always available for, and perhaps that is why we fail to take full advantage of the opportunity. Perhaps it's hard for us to embrace what an astonishing gift is being offered. We figure if it's really that easy to do, then how could it be that powerful? That's how much we underestimate how important we are to God.

In choosing not to listen for Him, we are choosing not to hear Him. For God's voice is a whisper, not a shout. Legend has it that when the angels came to the Virgin Mary in the middle of the night, they told her to get out of bed and go up to the roof. There they would reveal the extraordinary destiny that was to be hers. She had to go on to the roof in order to receive their message, the roof symbolizing her higher mind. If they had merely told her to sit up in bed, her mind and body still close to sleep, then she would not have been able to hear them. We too must be in a heightened, awakened state if we wish to hear the voice of God. Certain insights come to us after five or ten or twenty minutes of meditation, which simply do not emerge from the shallow waters of normal waking consciousness. Setting our mental focus within deeper waters in the morning helps ensure that our mind will remain there throughout the day.

The story of Mary's annunciation is the beginning of the Christ story and, like all beginnings, sets the energy for what will come. Her deep surrender to the will of God was the original opening through which God revealed Himself. Whether it's the beginning of a life or the beginning of a day, energies become set and hardened then; once a pattern is off and running, it's more difficult to change.

Time spent in morning prayer and meditation can save hours of tears shed later over something we have said or done. How many times have we said to ourselves, "How could I have been so dumb?" The answer is that we are not dumb; we were simply at the mercy of a frantic mind, not centered on its own sublime power. We were focused on things that are ultimately unimportant, while the deeper issues of life were left mainly ignored. These are the things that are bound to happen when we do not take the time each day to purify our thoughts.

According to *A Course in Miracles,* five minutes spent with God's Spirit in the morning guarantees He will be in charge of our thought forms throughout the day. Each morning we can begin with spiritual confidence, surrendering to God's will and praying that our eyes be opened to the miracles He has planned for us. Each day can be a glorious canvas painted by the hand of God, and we pray for eyes with which to see it.

Every morning, visualize and pray for divine right order: If you are a teacher, for instance, bear witness with your inner eye to an angel, or Jesus, or Buddha, wrapping his arms around every child in your class, then allow your mind to hold that image for five minutes or more. See God's Light around your coworkers, your neighbors, your children, your spouse. Whatever it is you will be doing with your day—whatever your workplace or activity—consciously bless the people you'll meet, as well as those you don't even know. Remember to include those you don't like as well as those you do. Allow yourself to imagine, while in a prayerful, meditative state, the life you most long to experience. Then bless that image, and surround it with light.

Now you can leave the house smiling, because you've placed your future in the hands of God. You've helped set the universe on a harmonious trajectory. Every day we have a chance to re-create life, for ourselves and others, reshaping our energies with the thoughts we think, just as we reshape our bodies with physical exercise. Bless the house in which you wake, and the people who also sleep there. Bless your city and your country and your world. Bless everyone you will meet today. Bless everyone else who is driving along the freeway with you. Ask that your mind be filled with light, that you might be a channel for God's love. You cannot do this regularly in a committed way and feel like your life has no purpose. When you give love you will feel love. That is Law.

Some days are harder than others, to be sure. Perhaps some of your mornings have gone like this: "There is no way I can do this. I'm supposed to go to Chicago, and my daughter is having her dance recital tonight. If I can't get home on the three-o'clock flight, which I probably won't because my meeting isn't until one, then I will miss her recital and be a terrible parent."

Now commit this truth to memory: There is no problem that holiness will not solve. No matter what the problem is, no matter how big or small, important or unimportant, you are entitled to a miracle because you are a child of God.

Using only our mortal minds, we have very little power to fix anything. The world is full of confusion, it is moving too fast, and the demands of parenthood, career, economics, and health are proving too stressful for almost everyone. But you're equipped with more than just your mortal mind. Within each of us there is a divine mind, the Mind of God. It is always there, with no exception, to work whatever miracle is necessary to lift us above the limitations of the world.

In *A Course in Miracles*, it is written, "Prayer is the conduit of miracles." There is no prayer too big or too small that we should withhold it from God.

So try this instead, on such a morning: "Dear God, please give me a miracle. I don't know how I'm going to go to Chicago and still get back to my daughter's recital. This life is so full of stress, dear God. Please take my day and plan it for me. Take care of her, and take care of me. Thank you, God. Amen."

Everything in the universe is of concern to God, since He loves everything as one. If you're too stressed, then you're not fully alive, and your problem is therefore very much

God's business. If you're not fully alive, then you're not being who you were born to be or living the life you are meant to live. If you're not living the life you are meant to live, then you're not doing on this earth what you're intended to do— you're failing to take part in the unfolding drama of infinite good, which is the spirit of God. If you're not being the parent you are capable of being, then another child is set up to fail. Why wouldn't a loving God wish to correct that situation? We are told in *A Course in Miracles* that we do not ask God for too much, but for too little. Every need we have should be placed in His hands.

The moment a mistake—any deviation from love—occurs, a perfect, all-knowing God has already planned a correction. All we have to do is ask that it be revealed to us. "Dear God, please show me a miracle."

We take spiritual responsibility for our day when we pray that it be blessed. More than the way we look, more than the clothes in our closet, more than whether or not our papers are organized, this simple request—that our lives be reflections of an eternal love—releases us from the confines of yesterday and frees us to unlimited possibilities today. Every single morning we can receive from the universe an entirely new day, in every sense of the word. Our ego will screech, "Denial!" should we have the audacity to consider the possibility of a radically new life today. Yet that's exactly what is available to us, and courage lies in claiming it.

Every morning, consider doing this: Light a candle. Sit down. Close your eyes. Be with God.

There are many different prayer and meditation techniques, and they are all paths to God. It matters not which path we walk to Him, but only *that we walk it*. In whatever way suits you, talk to God.

*Dear God,*
*I give you this morning.*
*Please take away*
*My despair of yesterday.*
*Help me to forgive the things*
*That caused me pain*
*And would keep me bound.*
*Help me to begin again.*
*Please bless my path*
*And illumine my mind.*
*I surrender to You*
*The day ahead.*
*Please bless every person*
*And situation*
*I will encounter.*

*Make me who You would have me be,*
*That I might do as You would have me do.*
*Please enter my heart*
*And remove all anger,*
*Fear and pain.*
*Renew my soul*
*And free my spirit.*
*Thank you, God,*
*For this day.*
*Amen.*

# 9:00 am

# Hearing the News

*You read the paper or watch the news on TV.*
*You learn about terrorist attacks, pedophile*
*priests, corporate greed and irresponsibility,*
*homicides, the destruction of our ecosystems,*
*horrible injustices, lack of airline safety,*
*and more, on any given day. . . .*
Right, *you think to yourself.*
So much for miracles. . . .

It is a spiritual challenge to hear the news and still keep your faith.

Surrounded by terrible news, we are tempted to feel powerless before the strength of darkness. And yet we are *not* powerless, for we are children of an infinitely wealthy father who has shared with us the prosperity of His kingdom. Our primary task is to remember that it's ours. Through God, we have the power to use our spiritual resources to banish all darkness—to transform our world from a state of limitation and fear to a state of abundance and love. For the world is a reflection of humanity's collective consciousness, and each of us has access to the collective through the auspices of our own mind.

Viewing life through the eyes of the world, we learn about a world that *is*; viewing life through the eyes of spirit, we learn about a world that *could be*. It is a law of consciousness that what we think about expands: Our focus amounts to a mental endorsement of the wordview that keeps the object of our focus in place. In order to change the world, we must change the mental lens through which we view it.

What is not love, according to *A Course in Miracles,* is a call for love. And according to the Jewish precept of *tikkun olam,* we are on this earth to heal the broken pieces of the world. The mystic views any problem as a chance to use his or her magic wands.

Think of the news as humanity's prayer list. How different the world would be if every day's newspaper reports were met with prayers for healing from its readers! And that will happen, when the modern mind realizes the power of spirit. Prayer itself will emerge from the constricting limitations of religious doctrine, to become a spontaneous call of the soul to the higher power from whence we came. Having claimed the dimension of power that spiritual wisdom provides, we will energetically engage in the process of creating a new civilization. We will no longer stand powerless before the so-called strength of illusion and fear; once we realize our spiritual power, we will assume it to its full degree. For through God, we have the power of the sun and the moon and the stars at our command.

Bless everyone mentioned in every news story, no matter where they stand or what they do. For what we bless is delivered to divine right order. Bless those who do harm as well as those who do good, for any judgment blocks the light and keeps miracles at bay. Becoming emotionally reactive when we are confronted with darkness only serves to keep the darkness alive. Reacting to fear with fear merely feeds the fear.

Instead, let us claim for ourselves the power of love. Read about war? Pray to be a peacemaker. Read about abused children? Pray to be an advocate for them. Read about corruption? Pray to be an active citizen who does his or her part to change that. Read about a reign of terror? Pray to see a loving world that exists in a realm beyond it, and for God to make you a significant part of the effort to bring it forth.

We invoke another world first by simply accepting that it is there. It's not something to be created, so much as something to be *recognized*. And that recognition *is* the miracle. Pure harmony *already* exists in the Mind of God, along with a blueprint for its emergence into the world. When our hearts and minds are realigned with His, then that world will naturally come forth. Regardless of what the newspapers or the television news might declare as the latest disaster, our job is to remain loyal to an emergent reality developing in the fertile ground of our passion and imagination. With faith in possibilities as yet unseen, we can *proclaim* the world we wish to see, and not take the ego's "no" for an answer. It is a basic metaphysical truth that no lie can last forever.

The level of disaster now occurring throughout the world leaves us looking for answers that ordinary human consciousness cannot provide. A catastrophe can be a wake-up call to the human race; it's only when we have truly awakened to the limits of mortal consciousness that we awaken at long last to the miracles of God.

Transcendence is a universal spiritual theme, and no religion has a monopoly on the idea that in God we are lifted above the limits of the world. One does not have to be Christian, for instance, to embrace the concept of the resurrection of spirit. In claiming the resurrection as a universal reality, we realize that our lives too can be lifted into a deathless dimension above the consciousness of the mortal world.

Darkness penetrates the human experience, but our response need not be frightened or weak. Our task is not to avoid or deny the darkness of the world, but to lift it into the light. We certainly don't want to live in denial, but there is negative denial and positive denial. Negative denial is when we ignore the darkness, claiming that since only love is real and all else is illusion, we need not dwell on the problems in our midst. But positive denial is something else: We do look at the darkness, yet we deny its power over us. Our function is not to ignore the darkness, but to transform it *by becoming the light*. The spiritual activist doesn't dwell on what's wrong, but at the same time we must know what's wrong in order to surrender it. Our miraculous authority lies in *positive* denial: *denial of the power of darkness by knowing that only light is the ultimate Reality*.

We are born of an extraordinary light, and have within our hearts the tools we need to rise above this world, to transform our suffering and that of others. We can consciously and courageously claim a different experience for this planet. But only if we are ready to commit to change. Just as the alcoholic must come to accept that alcohol cannot be part of his or her life anymore, we must all come to accept that thought forms of separation and fear—with their inevitably violent results—have no place on this planet anymore; they are too dangerous to the survival of the species. When love and forgiveness replace blame and retribution, we will have begun construction on a new and better world.

Children starve by the tens of thousands on this planet every day. They starve not because they have to but because we allow them to, and decisions that each of us make every day affect their plight. People do not dwell in poverty for no reason; they are poor because of conditions over which all of us exert some control. And as long as love is not our top priority, we will continue to manifest a world of pain. Only when we make love the basis of all our institutions will the news begin to change. And *that* will be our miracle.

When I read or watch the news, my biggest temptation is to judge those who disagree with me. The prayer that often pops into my mind, after reading the newspaper or listening to a television news show, goes something like this: "Dear God, please remove from my mind my sense that I'm right and other people are wrong, my temptation to feel contempt toward those I disagree with, and this feeling of complete and utter powerlessness with my sense that the world is falling apart. Help me to forgive. And use me, if possible, that I might help to make things better. Amen."

When I read about corporations who wage inappropriate influence on the government because of large campaign donations, I feel disgust. "What do you *mean,* the Vice President met with ninety-six energy executives, and not one environmentalist group?!" I fly into a rage. And while my ego is fine with that, my heart knows better than to indulge my self-righteousness. I know that rage will never solve anything. My spirit seems to whisper to me, "Fine. Fly off the handle if you want to. But be clear that it won't help the situation."

I imagine a conversation between my ego and my heart:

"So what am I supposed to do? Just *forgive* all those people who are destroying the planet?"

"Actually, yes."

*"Why?* They're ruining America! They would destroy the environment, and they're destroying democracy."

"I know this is difficult. Tell me what you're feeling right now."

"Obviously, I'm angry."

"And what is the feeling behind that feeling? What do you feel, in the deepest place within you?"

"I feel sad. I feel dreadfully, deeply sad. And I feel frightened."

"Frightened of what?"

"Frightened that my daughter and her children will only have polluted air to breathe, impure food to eat, and toxic water to swim in. I'm frightened that they won't even have a real democracy anymore, or enough rights to protect them should they choose to complain."

"And that is the point, you see. At the deepest level, you're not angry; you are sad and afraid. *Feel that.*"

Feeling our sadness and fear is actually more difficult

than exploding in anger, yet it's essential if we are to become the spiritual activists who can re-create the world. We must see with total clarity that what is not love is fear. And we must understand that every negative emotion therefore derives from fear. When we allow ourselves to feel the fear and sadness that lie behind our anger, our judgments undergo an extraordinary transformation, and our fury turns into compassion. This is an important issue if we really want to change the world. We have no morally persuasive power with people who can feel our underlying contempt. We cannot communicate in meaningful ways with those whom we approach with judgment or blame.

My heart asks, "What do you think about those people now?"

"I think they don't know what they're doing. I don't think they're bad. They just don't see what they're doing."

"And who are they to you?"

"They are my brothers. They are evolving spirits, and now I can see that they are my teachers. They are forcing me to open my heart and become bigger than my anger."

"Good. You're glimpsing your spiritual victory. Before, you were self-indulgent—which is exactly what you thought of them. And that made you part of the problem, not part of the solution. Your job is to seek your own atonement."

"Thanks for the guidance." Busted.

How we react to news affects our power to influence it. Too often in America, those who are most sensitive to the injustices in our midst allow themselves to be whiny and angry, thus limiting their capacity to create meaningful change. It's important to realize how much our emotional state can negatively affect the quality of energy we express to those around us, regardless of how "right" or "wrong" we might be. Once again, the process is as important as the goal. Taking responsibility for our own internal state is key to working miracles.

I try to remember the wands as I read the paper or watch the news. I want to remember that miracles do happen, that we are becoming people in whose presence these problems will melt, that my judgments help no one, that I must *be* the change I wish to see happen, and that at any given moment I can stop and pray, inviting God's spirit to enter both my heart and my mind. Then I have done my part to change things, for prayer brings a blessing to everyone and everything. For myself, I am then ready to receive whatever instruction God might give me, that I might be of use to Him in His efforts to heal the world.

Often, we are guided to do something to make the world a better place. Often, we are inspired to pray without ceasing. Almost always, we are moved to do both.

# 10:00 am

# Working

*You would rather be anywhere than going into this meeting. You think about being at the movies, being on the beach, being with your kids—being anywhere but here. The people waiting on the other side of that door don't know who you are or even seem to care. You don't have the feeling they really want you to succeed.*
*You can't believe you work here.*
*Welcome to your career. . . .*

American life today is centered on the workplace. The average adult spends more time each day with his or her employers or employees than with his or her partner, spouse, or children. Emotionally, our lives might center on our families and friends, but in terms of sheer time and energy, we spend most of our resources trying to make it at work.

Work, for many of us, is full of tension, anxiety, and pressure—with a bit of boredom and frustration thrown in. The average workday is a less-than-sacred experience, to be sure. So how do we transform the area of work from a material-based focus—with all its psychological and emotional pain—to an experience of spiritual freedom and joy?

A mystic takes every circumstance back to its spiritual foundation, asking fundamental questions about our higher identity and purpose. Who am I? Why am I here? What is the ultimate meaning of my life, my relationships, my work? If life is to have deeper meaning, can our work be something we merely do to make money? Or can work itself become sacred, a channel through which we shine our light and extend our love?

Ministry is not just for ministers: In the new spirituality, a minister is anyone who chooses to use our resources to tend to the wounded heart of the world. Anything we do can be a ministry, from menial labor to the highest professional endeavor. It is our ministry if it is an activity we use to spread peace and forgiveness and love.

We transform our work into a sacred experience by transforming our sense of its purpose—from that of serving our own needs as we define them to that of serving the work of God. This shift in purpose—from a focus on ourselves to a focus on God's love—activates a chain of miracles. For anytime we walk into a situation with a higher sense of why we are there, we are bringing down the light.

The decision to adjust our perspective on a situation, seeing as its only purpose the extension of love, automatically illumines it. For a situation to be illumined, our *thoughts* must become illumined. Within this light, our ideas are more insightful and wise, our personal energies radiate integrity, and circumstances around us unfold along a palpable path of divine right order. There is a "flow" we can all feel when a situation is aligned with the peace of God.

We should not have to *choose* between being in the flow of God's love and having a successful career. Indeed, the former fosters the latter. Yet in our society, it's very easy to buy in to the ego's perspective on employment and career. The ego represents the belief in our own, small, separated self, and sustains its life by defending that belief. And this belief fosters fear, because it is not a belief that is natural to us. We then seek to overcome that fear by building up our own individual kingdoms of money or prestige or power. We are often faced with the temptation to build our own career wins on someone else's losses. But once we realize that we are not separate from others, that indeed what we do to others we are literally doing to ourselves, then our perspective changes.

When we remember who we *really* are, we embrace our interconnectedness with all of life and the infinitude of our powers. We aren't here just to bolster our individual kingdoms; we are here to glorify God's kingdom of love. As children of God, we are natural storehouses of talent and intelligence; creativity flows from us like mother's milk, when our consciousness is that of mother to a new world. Once we change our consciousness of work from self-centered ambition to love-centered service, we begin to experience the effortless flow of divine inspiration.

I was given a prayer candle by a girlfriend, with a prayer called "The Goddess Within of Victories and Successes." When I begin my writing day by lighting that candle, praying that the work I do be of use to God, then my nervous system responds with a sense of focus and clarity I do not otherwise have. If I begin my writing thinking about contracts, money, or bestseller status, then I'm trapped in the illusions of the ego, where my thoughts are fragmented and my focus limited. Only when I begin with a prayer that something I write might be of use to someone does a greater light infuse my thinking. My mind opens vibrantly to its natural talents, sprung free of its bondage to fear-based thought.

An attitude of giving will ultimately attract more material and spiritual wealth to us than will an attitude of getting. But it takes faith in the workings of the spiritual universe to trust that this is so. The voice of the ego is loud, but its message is a lie. Pursuing success for nothing but personal gain will not and cannot lead to true joy, because it is a quest that is out of harmony with the ultimate reality of the universe.

In the movie *A Beautiful Mind,* the character John Nash

makes a discovery that Adam Smith was not completely correct when he argued that capitalism works at its best when everyone does what is best for them. Rather, argued Nash, it works best when everyone does what is best for them *and* best for the group.

A business dynamic that puts short-term economic gain for corporate CEOs or their shareholders before the welfare of the people who work in the company and live on this planet is based on fear, not love. The proper role of business is to minister—not to exploit. Whether as an employee or an employer—and many of us are both—it is our job, as bearers of light, to transform an ethos of control, suppression, and competition into an ethos of sharing, creativity, and joy.

Remember, it's not just workers but *souls* who are gathered in the workplace; we're not just here to "achieve" in a worldly sense, but to spiritually learn and grow. *That* is the purpose of work, because it is the ultimate purpose of everything. The ego's work drama is always centered on who does what, who works for whom, and how much money can be made. But beneath the ego's drama lies a deeper set of issues.

If we are the employer, then our spiritual lesson is that we learn to lead with compassion and respect for the output of others. If we are the employee, then our spiritual lesson is that we learn to serve and respect another's vision. And if spiritual transgression is no less significant when it occurs at work than anywhere else, then many values dominating the modern workplace are called into fundamental question.

The ego's bottom line in business is that as much money be made as possible this quarter, the project be finished by deadline, the sales of the department be increased, etc. Yet once we've taken on the mantle of mystic, we are committed to the furtherance of life and the revelation of spirit. This doesn't mean that we lower our standards of excellence; it means simply that we remember that the process is as important as our goal. *How* we do business is as important as the business we do. We are not just concerned with how business operates; we are concerned with how the universe operates. And we are not just concerned with what the market wants; we are concerned with what *God* wants. Love becomes our new bottom line.

Imagine how differently American business would function were our faith in the power of goodness to replace our faith in the power of money. Huge industries would no longer make billions of dollars on activities that diminish the well-being and safety of our children, our health, and our environment, on the pretext that it's "just business." To put money before goodness is idolatry, and the laws of the universe ensure that in the end all idols will fall.

Within the workplace, we've known for years that

money alone does not increase people's productivity. It's the feelings of respect, honor, and involvement that make people realize their highest potential. Both as an employer and as an employee, I've seen how very true this is. As an employer, it's obvious to me that work doesn't get done just because I say that it must be done. How I say something is critical; often, the energy behind my comment is even more important than what I say. Ultimately, it's only people who have done and continue to do their own inner work who can effectively lead a competent modern workplace. As an employee, it's equally obvious to me that I don't produce just because someone tells me to produce, but rather because positive reinforcement and encouragement help my creative juices flow. When I'm intimidated, it does not make me more productive; when I'm criticized, I shut down. The role of a leader is not to rule over other people, but to hold a space for their own genius.

Work goes better when we connect to our common humanity first and our common professional goals second. When it's the other way around, we are not aligned with spiritual truth, and therefore chaos rather than harmony prevails. We are always working alongside the children of God, and all of us contain within us the love of our divine source. When we spend five minutes every morning blessing everyone with whom we work, seeing them held in the arms of

God, then our workplace cannot help but transform. When we pray before a business meeting—asking that it be graced by God's love and that we be instruments of His will—then the meeting will be blessed.

Still, both employees and employers often have very valid complaints: How can I work for someone who doesn't show me enough respect? And how can I respect an employee who has such a sense of entitlement and does mediocre work? Spirit does not suppress those questions, but creates a context in which they can be harmoniously and effectively addressed.

From a spiritual perspective, if we have a disrespectful employee *or* a disrespectful employer, the situation is there for a reason. If someone feels we aren't showing them enough respect, then probably, on some level, we are not. And if someone feels we're not performing at our best, then probably, on some level, we are not. It is our own thoughts— not someone else's—that hold the key to miraculous transformation. What am I not giving that needs to be given to my employer or my employee? What am I not seeing that needs to be seen in the effort of my employer or employee? And what am I not saying that needs to be said to my employer or my employee? Asking ourselves these questions can deeply affect the workplace. People who have not done their internal work—whose subconscious unresolved issues are projected constantly onto those around them—are difficult to deal with as employees and employers as well. But essentially we are all the same, with the same hopes and dreams. We wish to be both respected and honored, and that is as true in the workplace as anywhere else.

Our modern culture has placed work and business in a dry and almost soulless context, where our deeper human needs are second to the needs of an economic machinery. Feeling no deeper acknowledgment of our own humanity, we can become insensitive to the humanity of those whose lives our businesses affect. Often no one, from the CEO down, feels free to question the basic morality of a business decision. People sit with unspoken concerns about safety and ethics eating away at them, afraid to protest lest they endanger their jobs.

Can we really be all *that* amazed at the revelation of corruption in the Enron scandal? That particular drama is nothing more or less than the logical extension of the business values we've allowed to prevail over the last few decades. Many have lost their moral compass amidst the materialism and greed of our times. And can any of us honestly say that we ourselves have never been tempted to put first things second and second things first?

Let us stop and give ourselves time to reenvision our work and rethink its mission. The vast majority of people want to do good. We want to feel that we're contributing to something bigger than ourselves. Whether we are the CEO of a large company or the person who cleans the office building, we are made up of the same essential stuff. Compassion for each other and the world we are here to serve will open up new vistas of productivity and abundance for us all.

Compassion in the workplace does not mean we should lower our standards, acquiesce to the violation of boundaries, or indulge a sloppy performance. It does mean, however, recognizing that in God's world no one is above and no one is below. That does not mean that no one gets to be the boss or that leadership should not be respected. It simply means that the salute of one soul to another should be at the core of every relationship. We all get off the track at times; certainly I know that I do. But I also know that getting back on that track is essential if my spirit and my work are to thrive.

Shifting the American workplace from a hierarchical structure of domination and competition to a new paradigm system of cooperation and partnership is a spiritual challenge for our generation. From more enlightened work relationships will emerge more enlightened goals; we will no longer abuse the planet when we no longer abuse one another. We will work to re-create our society in the image of our better

selves, and then we will know that the meaning of work, and
the joy of work, lie in dedicating our work to God.

*Dear God,*
*I surrender to you my work.*
*May I be who you would have me be,*
*That I might do as you would have me do.*
*May my relationships be blessed,*
*With those for whom I work*
*And with those who work for me.*
*May Your light be upon us*
*As we do our work,*
*And may our work*
*Be Yours.*
*Amen.*

# 11:00 am

# Needing Work

*At first, the articles in the paper don't seem to apply to you. Sure, there are problems, but they don't seem to be hitting too hard around here. Then the rumors begin. . . . And the boss is looking the other way when you pass in the hall. You can feel it in your gut: "This job is not as secure as I thought." And then it happens, just as you feared it would. It's you. . . . It's your desk. . . . It's your job. It's gone.*

During the last months of 2001, the Ford Motor Company announced they would be laying off 35,000 North American workers, Enron collapsed in the largest corporate bankruptcy in American history, and the United States fell into a recession. Behind every statistic of a laid-off worker or an investor who had lost their life savings lay human anxiety, desperation, and fear. How many of us have lost our jobs, moved on from our jobs without knowing if the risk was worth it, or had a parent or partner who went through that experience?

Jobs are not mere statistics to the people who hold

them. Our jobs are one of the means by which we contribute to society. They are the means by which we provide for our families. They are the means by which we pay our rent, and feed, clothe, and educate our children. When our jobs disappear, our self-esteem often disappears with them; when the money disappears, fear enters fast. In the United States today—while things are very good for some—there are many for whom financial stress is a daily heartache.

The mystic's first recourse when we are stressed is to take a step back and view the situation from a cosmic perspective. How do we do this, when circumstances affect us in such significant ways? There is a kind of spiritual muscle we develop, which gives us the strength to visualize any situation surrounded by light and embraced in the arms of God. Our mystical power lies in knowing that any situation can be seen through different eyes, and that our choice to see a situation differently is an invitation for miracles to enter. God will do His part when we do ours. The work of resurrection is a continuous process, at work in all dimensions of time and space. Where there is lack, God's abundance is on the way. Hold on. Have faith. It's coming.

When we've lost a job, our mystical strength lies in not buying into the appearance of lack. Our emotions naturally run high, and it's important that we feel them. But spiritual victory lies in saying to any condition that does not reflect

God's perfection, "Get behind me. I know you're not real, even though it feels like you are." From this conviction flows a miraculous elixir that alchemizes our emotions and brings them, in time, into alignment with God's reality. It takes time for one condition to transform into another, and during that time our consciousness is crucial. In denying the unreal, we call forth the Real.

The ego looks only to the externals: get a new résumé, call this person or that person, arrange for unemployment insurance, etc. All of that and more might be called for on the worldly plane. But it is a mistake to look to God as a last resort, second to more practical solutions. He is not, after all, a mere weak appendage to the really powerful things we can do to help ourselves. Our greatest power lies in asking God to light our way.

Do not pose for God, but rather be real: It is a good idea to present our pain to Him exactly as we feel it. We might pray, "Dear God, I need a job. I give to You all of the emotions I feel about this . . . my grief . . . my fear . . . my humiliation. I know there were things I should have done differently. I am ashamed of myself; I don't know how to face my kids; I'm afraid no one will hire me, that I'm not good enough." Whatever we actually feel should form the crux of our communication to God; He is, as Stevie Wonder sings, "the only free psychiatrist that's known throughout the world." We have to be honest with God, both about our pain and our shortcomings, in order for His spirit to enter us in the deepest places and transform us. According to *A Course in Miracles,* He cannot take from us what we will not release to Him.

We can lose a job and still know we have a career. We can lose money and still retain a consciousness of wealth. We can lose the things of this world, but the knowledge of our connection to God is something no one can take away. It's ours to remember if we choose to remember it. Place the shame, the humiliation, the fear in the hands of God. Literally pray it away. We can allow God's spirit to deliver us from the emotions that reflect our disappointment to the emotions that reflect our hope and joy.

Seekers are aware that in the mortal world, things come and go. And that's why we wish to keep our emotional center of gravity elsewhere. We choose to remain in the House of the Lord—the energy of divine consciousness—both when the money and job are happening, and when the money and job are not happening. When money is here, it behooves us to remain humble, grateful, and devoted to service. When money is not here, remember that we live in God, work in God, lean on God, and will rise back up in God. Anything can increase our connection to Him if we allow it to, and often it is the situations that take us to our knees that take us home to Him.

From a spiritual perspective, while we can lose our earthly employment, we cannot lose the job God gave us. We are the permanent holders of a spiritual career, for it is what we are and not just what we do that represents our greatest work in the world. As long as we remain vigilant at building our internal abundance—an abundance of integrity, an abundance of forgiveness, an abundance of service, an abundance of love—then external lack is bound to be temporary.

So what's important is to remember that your first job on earth is to be a minister of God, whether you're employed or unemployed as the world defines it. We cannot be unemployed if we are employed by God Himself. We are on this earth to do a job for Him, to be about our Father's business, to become whom He would have us be, that through Him we might extend into the universe the love that will save the world. This is not a job that is given and then taken away. It is the opportunity inherent in every moment. As long as there are ways we can serve, then we have a job to do. Love and forgiveness form our mission on earth, and that is why they are key to our emotional well-being. In God's Reality, we cannot lose that job. God will not fire us, and His business cannot fail.

Appearances to the contrary exist only to challenge us, tempting us to place our faith in illusions. Having forgotten who we really are—suffering from illusions about our own identity—our perceptions of the world are doomed to be illusory as well. But as our sense of self is repaired, our illusions fall away. In remembering who we are in relation to God, we remember who we are in relation to each other and to the world around us. From the miracle of our realignment with God flows every other miracle we need. God's spirit is a heavenly consciousness of divine oneness, always beckoning you to remember that there is nothing you can do, nothing that can happen, that can ever lessen your eternal value in His eyes. You have tremendous gifts to give; God sent them with you when you came to this earth. And while you might forget them, or doubt that they exist, God does not forget and He will show them to you. As soon as your gifts are dedicated to His work, they will blossom. Chains that might have held you back for years will dissolve. And you will feel free. You will learn that your spirit is bigger than your circumstances, as soon as you put your spirit first.

If you have lost your job, then another situation, just as good or better, already exists in the Mind of God. It can be difficult to feel this way when stress is high, but our feelings are not always perfect indicators of reality. The infinite, unalterable power of God is such that whenever something contrary to His love is introduced into the universe, a miraculous alternative automatically develops. We pray that our eyes might be open, that we might see what has already happened. When we pray for God to illumine our path, we are saying, "Dear God, please show me the way. What thoughts do I need to think, to be able to navigate my life at this point? What perceptions do I need; what insights will guide me? Who do I need to forgive? What parts of my personality do I need to look at; what changes do I need to make? Please come upon me and heal my life. Amen."

In God's world, there is only abundance, regardless of what we are experiencing within our human drama. The remembrance of our mystical identity will restore our confidence, reminding us that we're part of that abundance. Lack is a temporary condition, often reflecting a fractured sense of self: Thinking we were small, we acted in a small way and now reap the effects of our self-limiting thoughts or behavior. Material abundance will not restore a broken sense of self, but a restored sense of self will attract whatever abundance we need.

On a spiritual plane, "having" and "being" are synonymous. The greatest form of abundance is to remember who we are: that we are literally part of the abundance of the universe. Usually our experience of material lack reflects our failure to allow ourselves the hugeness of that realization.

Our greatest need is for the hand of God to build a bridge over which we can cross from mortal perception to divine understanding. Our prayer is not simply, "Dear God, please send me a better job," but, "Dear God, enable me to see this situation differently, that this area of apparent lack might be healed inside my mind." There is only ever one problem: that we are separated somehow from the thinking of God.

Miracles can come from anything, anywhere, anytime. There is no situation that ties God's hands. He is bigger than layoffs, or recessions, or stock market losses. Every ending is a new beginning. Through the grace of God, we can always start again.

You have not been fired; you have been liberated. You might not feel that way, which is fine. Cry your tears, but remember this: The resurrected state already exists. It lives within us all as an eternal and operative principle. Claim your good, for it is on the way.

If you allow this situation to throw you more deeply into the arms of God, then the next time someone hires you—and they will—they will be hiring someone who is better at what you do because you are more fully who you are. Fear comes, but fear passes. Only the truth of who you are remains, to shine on everything. And that is your job, now and always: to shine and thus illumine the world.

# 12:00 Noon

# Being Happy

*It was her third birthday, and we had the party in the backyard. There were lots of children and lots of games, and Cinderella arrived just before we cut the cake. My daughter's jaw dropped open at the sight of Cinderella gliding across the grass. "Mommy, you got her to come over to our house?" she exclaimed. Her eyes were wide and as sparkly as Cinderella's rhinestone tiara.*
*Later she asked me in a whisper,*
*"Is Barbie here, too?"*

I have learned from experience that happiness is an acquired skill. There is always something to complain about, even in the best of times. And there is always something to celebrate, even in the worst of times. Happiness is not an objective reality so much as a subjective decision. Chronic complainers miss the boat.

Many people are addicted to suffering and have a mental habit of pointing out the worst in people or situations. Not only are they robbing themselves of joy, but their failure to appreciate all the goodness that life has to offer actually diminishes that good. Both our blessing and our condemnation have power. Thinking that something is bad has the power to make it so in our experience.

Children are one of our greatest lessons in happiness, constantly challenging us to enjoy the moment, as the next one will not be the same. There is no sense saying about a small child, "Well, I'll enjoy watching her at the beach splashing around in the waves, but I'll do it later, next year or the next year." Next year, she will not splash around in the same way. Two years old gives way to three and then four. And before you know it there is a teenager standing in front of you who won't even *want* to go to the beach with you. You'll wonder where all the years went, but they will be gone. No more watching her finger paint. She doesn't finger paint anymore.

I have lived large parts of my life in wonderful circumstances that I utterly failed to appreciate. Reasons to be happy were everywhere, but somehow I didn't connect with them. It was as though I was eating but couldn't taste the food. Finally, I've learned to celebrate the good while it's happening. I feel gratitude and praise today for what are sometimes such simple pleasures. I have learned that happiness is not determined by circumstances. Happiness is not what happens when everything goes the way you think it should go; happiness is what happens when you decide to be happy.

There was a time a few years ago when several members

of my family died in quick succession. It seemed as though all we did was go to funerals, gathering together to cry. Then, several years later, Hilary, the oldest of my late sister's daughters, got married. Finally, we were gathering not to grieve but to celebrate, and the gratitude everyone felt was palpable. Every living member of Hilary's family came to the wedding, from many places around the world, and all of us knew why. We would have loved her and celebrated her marriage even if her mother and her grandfather and her uncle had not recently died. But everyone knew that the circumstances of the last few years made this wedding, this *mitzvah,* even more important. The event was so infinitely sweet because it contrasted dramatically with the bitterness of the previous few years.

So those who have learned to be happy are often those who have suffered most. When simple pleasures have been taken away, such as someone's loving smile or encouraging word, then the next time such pleasures come around—and they do—we lift our cup of life to them. We sing God's praises in a way we had never done in the days when we took so much for granted.

Gratitude is essential to happiness. Developing a grateful attitude—knowing that every time we arrive somewhere safely, we have something to be happy about; every time our children rush up to us and smile, we have something to be happy about; every time we get out of bed and can take a deep breath and go out for a walk, we have something to be happy about—that is the essence of a happy existence. Happiness is a muscle we must use, or it will wither away.

Whatever we focus on is bound to expand. Where we see the negative, we call forth more negative. And where we see the positive, we call forth more positive. Having loved and lost, I now love more passionately. Having won and lost, I now win more soberly. Having tasted the bitter, I now savor the sweet.

Several years ago, a friend of mine lived with me during the final few months of her life. Not completely understanding the effects of her illness, I kept saying, "Michelle, you must eat. You're getting too thin! Eat!" And after she died, I read in her journal about how "Marianne takes it for granted that if you eat, you gain weight; if you want to go out somewhere, you can; and if you want to live past this year, it's a reasonable proposition." She was someone who had so little to be happy about, but she taught me so much about happiness. During those months, right after the birth of my daughter, I would come home to find my dying friend with my baby snuggled next to her. There was a smile of bliss on both their faces that I will remember all my days.

# 1:00 pm

# Feeling Jealous

*You can't get a book contract, but someone else you know just had their first book hit number one on Amazon.com; you passed on the stock in your friend's new company, and everyone who bought in is a millionaire now; you've just broken up with the love of your life, and everywhere you look there's an issue of Modern Bride. Despite your best efforts, your skin is turning green. . . .*

We're all a little ashamed to admit our own loveless-ness when it comes to jealousy and envy. In a world that has constantly drilled into us a belief in scarcity, it seems that there are only so many pieces of the pie; if someone else gets a piece, we think there must be less for us.

But in God's universe, there is no scarcity. There is always "enough," because consciousness is endlessly creative. No one else's good fortune diminishes our own except when we choose to denigrate it. Only our own judgment can stop the flow of goodness to our door. Abundance is our spiritual birthright, which is ours to either receive or resist. Our blessing someone else's abundance only attracts abundance to us, just as judging those who have what we would like to have obstructs it.

None of us ever *want* to feel jealous, of course. It's a feeling that comes over all of us despite our best intentions. We feel we can't help it at times, when someone else gets the promotion, or the credit, or the relationship, or the money. . . . Their win can trigger primitive feelings of failure or loss, and the intellect has little or no power to assuage that pain. Mystics do not deny these negative emotions; we *surrender* them. We know we're feeling them for a reason, as they often represent the places in our psyche where we relive previous wounds within the context of current experience. The negative emotion we're feeling now—if we surrender it deeply and ask for God's healing—is our chance to transform the past and be free of its pain in the present.

While in the midst of our pain, we can reach for Truth—for the abstract principles by which we reinterpret our experiences in a more positive light. A tough mind is the greatest complement to a tender heart. Embracing God's Truth is a spiritual *act:* It alchemizes our emotions, providing the bridge from fear to love.

Think of the mystical "three days" between the crucifixion and the resurrection as the time it takes for a situation to change, once spirit has infused our consciousness. As we come to look at an experience differently, in time it begins to transform. The choice to perceive any situation within a spiritual context cuts through our negativity. Where we place our faith is critical. For we *do* live in a limitlessly abundant universe. And even when we feel loss and limitation, our choice to affirm what we know to be true—that we are limited by nothing—brings the power of Truth to bear on any situation. We can have faith in a world of limitation, or we can have faith in a world of limitless good. But it shall be given to us according to our faith: What we have *faith* in is what we will experience on some level.

I once had a friend who was a struggling actor. I was always impressed by how genuinely happy he was when one of his friends got a break. Regardless of any pain or disappointment he might have been feeling about his own career, he was always sincere in his congratulations for others. When his big break did come, I wasn't surprised. By celebrating the success of others, he helped draw success toward himself. I wondered if I could've done as well.

Years ago, I noticed that several women who had started out by attending my lectures were now giving talks to audiences of their own, appearing on television at times in places where I no longer did. And I did feel a little jealous. I had to feel those feelings and not deny them; the only negative feelings that have the power to hurt us are those that haven't been processed and surrendered. It's only when we put our hurt feelings into the fire of transformation—allowing ourselves to feel them and continuing to surrender them—that they finally begin to burn away. I prayed for those women and their continued success and, as time went on, my own thoughts and feelings began to transform. I learned so much from this, gaining insight into how I might have appeared to others when I was younger, and about how best to gracefully fill the role I have now.

Those women were newer on the scene—a little hotter, a little younger. But once I gave them that—grieving the role that I can no longer play and passing that torch along to them—I received the blessing of another realization. I saw that now I'm an elder of sorts in my professional community. I have a role to play as someone who *has* been around a while, and my niche today is every bit as significant as the niche that now belongs to them. But I had to let go of what had been mine in the past in order to receive what is mine today.

For women, it can be particularly hard to deal with physical jealousy in our society, which is so geared toward youth and beauty. Many women of my generation are grappling with this phenomenon in our middle years, having so glorified our own youth and set the precedent for its overemphasis. Younger women, whose skin still glows with a voluptuousness we naively thought would be ours forever, can be particularly hard to love and bless!

Now, we tell ourselves, we are older and wiser: we're becoming the elders and we should honor that role, society needs its elders, etc. But often, what we're really thinking is, "Yeah, I'm older and wiser, but I would rather look good! I know that society needs its elders, but I wish *I* wasn't one of them." We try to paste on a more politically correct consciousness, yet still we need to feel our authentic feelings or our healing will not be authentic either.

Often we're confronted by people who have something we used to have, or have something we never had and still want. There are often things to grieve in life, whether they be youth or lost opportunities or people who have moved on. And grief is an important step along the spiritual path, because only when we have fully grieved something can we completely let it go. Dreams often do die hard, and there is nothing negative about feeling their loss. Only when we have truly cried all our tears have we cleansed ourselves of the toxic barriers to the experience of genuine joy.

By surrendering to God's will, we receive so very much more than we would ever get by allowing jealousy to guide our thoughts and behavior. From acceptance and surrender at last there comes an awe-filled grace. And with grace comes the opening of our eyes. We begin to see that every circumstance and every situation is just a corner of an infinite universe. No corner is really so good or bad, as it is simply a place the soul is in need of experiencing now. Whatever it is, it will not last. Whatever it is, it is leading to something better. And whatever it is, it is actually perfect.

# 2:00 pm

# Making Decisions

*Maybe I should let my daughter go to the
school her friends are attending, or maybe
I should send her to the other one; maybe I
should take the job in San Francisco, or maybe
I should stay in Dallas; maybe I should keep
fighting to make this relationship work,
or maybe I should let it go. Making
decisions is the worst thing in the world.
Or maybe it's not; I can't decide. . . .*

Having to make decisions can be awful. We go round and round in our minds, not quite knowing which set of factors should be given greater weight. Sometimes reason competes with gut instinct, which only seems to make matters worse.

But what if we could place all our decisions in the hands of God? What if a decision surrendered to the divine was a decision surrendered to the highest level of intelligence, wisdom, and love?

We're not schooled by traditional modes of thinking to believe that such effortlessness is possible, and so we remain locked into the stress of making decisions about a future we cannot forecast. We stand before a bend in the road without knowing what's around the corner. Yet we are expected to make decisions about what *might* be there, decisions that could affect the rest of our lives.

Metaphysics is the study of the invisible forces that underlie our human experience. And God, according to metaphysical interpretations of religion, dwells in a realm that is separate from our human drama, in which the horrors and pain of this world do not exist. But He sends into this realm a divine ambassador, imbued with His power, to deliver us from fear to love. One of the names of that ambassador is the Holy Spirit.

Because the Holy Spirit is the part of our mind that remains in conscious contact with God, we can safely place all decisions in His hands. The mortal ego dwells in linear time and does not know the future; the Holy Spirit dwells in eternity and therefore *does.* He knows not only what will happen in the future, *but also how every decision made will affect every living thing forever.* Imagine an infinitely complex computer that could reliably analyze any situation and give a readout, to the nth detail, of what would happen if this, this, or that were to occur. We don't get to see the readout, of course, but we are given simple instructions on how best to behave in order to support the highest outcome for ourselves and others. The instructions might come in a form as simple as an intuitive flash, or a complex process of growth and understanding that gradually unfolds within us.

There have been situations where I made what turned out to be a wrong decision, and I had to experience the remorse that comes when we realize we've acted against our own instincts and now regret it. Often we receive a kind of "inner knowing" about something, yet we disregard that knowing because we can't rationally explain it. The more we pray, meditate, and take our spiritual practice seriously, the better listeners we become to the small, still voice for God. We come to understand that there are means of knowing beyond the rational. Now that I've fully realized how much smarter God is than I, and how willing He is to share what He knows, my life is much easier. It is not an abdication of responsibility, but rather the ultimate taking of responsibility, to ask God to do our thinking for us. He is not outside us, after all. He is the Mind of the realized Self.

Sometimes we'll wonder, "Should I have that meeting on Thursday or Friday?" We look at our calendar and see that Thursday is the less busy day, therefore the most rational day to set up the meeting—but something inside keeps saying, "Do it on Friday. . . ." So many times in my life I've gone with Thursday, only to have something happen later that made Thursday very much the wrong day. And Friday, of course, would have been perfect.

Sometimes Spirit speaks loudly and directly. A friend of mine was once deciding whether or not to run for mayor of his hometown. I knew he was going through a lot of questioning, trying to weigh all the various factors involved in making such a decision. One day he called to chat.

"So how is it going, Steve?" I asked him.

"Oh, it's such a whirlwind here," he said. "I don't know what to do. Bob Garner might run again for his Congressional seat, in which case I don't want to run against him. But he might not run because he might want to run for senator. The senator might not be running because he might want to come back here and run for governor. In the meantime, everyone keeps asking me to run for mayor, but I can't decide because I think maybe I should stay out of politics for another year or two and establish myself in the community first. Then again, I think maybe I should make the run for mayor, and I have to decide because the filing date is next week, but I keep going back and forth and it's driving me nuts."

It was driving me nuts, too, just listening to him. My head was whirling. "Steve," I said. "You're thinking about this in such a worldly way. Political strategizing tends to be very left brain and rationalistic. Have you considered making the decision about what to do from a spiritual perspective?"

"That would be great!" he said. "But how do I do that?"

"Just ask God to decide for you," I told him. "You can't possibly know what the future holds. You can't know all the various factors going on behind the scenes. So just ask God if He wants you to be in politics—if that's the best way you can serve Him—and that if it is, please let you know whether to run for mayor in this next election."

"That sounds great!" Steve said. And so we prayed. We placed his career, and this particular decision, in the hands of God.

"Thank you so much," he said, when we had finished the prayer. "I feel so much lighter."

After that, we got off the phone, and about fifteen minutes later my phone rang again. It was Steve.

"You won't believe what happened!" he exclaimed. "When I was talking to you, I was on the phone in my office, which is in a space behind my house. Right after we finished our call, I walked back into the house to get some coffee, and the minute I walked in, the phone rang. I picked it up, and it was the editor from our local newspaper. He was calling to give me a heads-up about an anonymous ad that was placed in his paper today, and that will be running in to-morrow's edition. It's a full page that simply says, 'Run, Steve, Run.' "

We giggled at the amazing serendipity, and after that, Steve certainly felt that he knew what he should do. I don't think he will ever forget that day, or doubt that God can answer his questions.

God's answers don't always come through as loudly or clearly as full-page newspaper ads, but they find their way to us nevertheless. Sometimes we don't hear an answer simply because we're not listening; we're not yet prayerful and meditative enough to have honed our spiritual "hearing." Sometimes we don't hear an answer because the answer lies in more fully living the question. And sometimes we hear exactly what God is telling us, but we are not yet prepared to own up to what we know. By cultivating a state of mind in which we place our decisions where they belong, in the hands of One who always knows what we should do, we draw on a mystical power no worldly means of decision-making can match. God will listen and God will answer, with a prescience and wisdom and intelligence and love for us and for everyone in the whole entire world.

# 3:00 pm

# Feeling Bored

*You have been on the freeway for an hour and
a half, and you are moving at perhaps twenty
miles an hour. The smog is thick and the air
is hot. This day is just the same old thing,
with no variety or enchantment or joy.
Will you be making this commute forever?
Is this what you were born to do? You
would have hoped your life was
more important than this. . . .*

Every day, millions of people commute long, boring hours to jobs they don't love and then go home to less than happy families. It's amazing how much time we spend on things that feel like wasted time.

The circumstances of our lives are not always exciting, yet they tend to change only when we do. The excitement we seek will not come from an external source, but only from an internal one. I have never known an exciting person who lived a really boring life. An exciting person makes a decision to live a more exciting way: to read substance instead of junk, to listen to books on tape instead of listening to bad radio, to engage in things that matter instead of frivolous pursuits.

Every moment, faithfully lived, is a chance to practice the art of living. A life of magnitude does not just happen; it is consciously chosen. Living is an endlessly creative process in which we work on achieving the life we want through our willingness to be who we would like to be.

Spiritually, there is a lesson in every moment: When we are seemingly stuck in a boring routine, the miracle lies not so much in finding something else to do as in realizing how much we can do in any single moment—through the power of our own consciousness—to transform ourselves and the world around us. According to *A Course in Miracles,* only what we are not giving can be lacking in any situation.

How many times are we tempted to say, "Well, this is just boring work, so I don't really need to show up for it fully. I don't need to be energetic, or excellent. It's really not an important job"? Yet when we say our job is boring, often we are merely indicating our unwillingness to show up fully for it. Failing to be a giver, we feel ungiven to. Failing to show up fully for life, our life then seems to feel empty.

If we give it just a minute's thought, we realize our lives are usually far, far better than those of billions of people around the world. In any given moment, someone is tortured, someone is starving, someone is dying a painful death or grieving for his or her most beloved. If people can rise above such things—and miraculously they do—then we can pick up our mystical wands and rise above the frustration of being stuck in traffic.

The frustration of traffic is a good metaphor for the frustration of modern life. We want to get somewhere. . . . But it's going too slow, and all these other people are in our way! If we wish to remain affected by traffic, or by anything else, then that's our choice. The day is hot, perhaps, and we have no air-conditioner, or the day is cold and we have no heater. We can think, *Poor me.* The drivers around us are acting nuts. We can think, *These people are total jerks.* We can think that way if we choose to, but we cannot diminish the power of our thoughts. Every thought of victimization or attack is an attack upon ourselves. When we think them, we are opening a door: enter stress, enter sickness, enter fear.

Using a mystical wand is a perceptual choice: In any given moment, we can reach for prayer the way some people reach for cigarettes or food. Prayer is a conscious decision to realign ourselves with divine right order, in the full awareness that without this realignment we are at the mercy of a chaotic world. And we need not be. The children of God are held back by nothing when we remember who we are.

And the only way to remember who we are is by also remembering who everyone else is. The drama of the material plane is an illusion that hides a truer Truth. The mystic has asked for new eyes, through which we see so much more than other people stuck in traffic with us, or on the subway with us, or in life with us. With mystical eyes, we see many other souls: hoping as we do, hurting as we do, trying their best from day to day just as we do. As we expand our understanding of their lives, we expand our experience of our own.

None of us, in our spiritual essence, is just a mortal creature, defined and limited by the material world. Rather, we are children of God who have been limited by nothing so much as the smallness of our story—the story we have told ourselves and believed when others have told us—that to be human is to be limited, powerless, or weak. It is not the transformation of our circumstances, but of our self-perception—from identifying with our limited bodies to our infinite spirits—that frees the world around us to sparkle with infinite possibilities.

You are free to experience life negatively or positively, and the choice you make determines whether you are at cause, or at effect, of the life you are living. You could be standing at your kitchen sink or sitting at your desk, sweeping your floor or painting a picture. It doesn't matter where you are or what you're doing; you could be in a castle by the sea, changing a baby's diaper, or living in a prison cell. Your mind is holy because you are a child of God, and now in this moment you have no higher purpose in life, nor will you ever, than to merely know that holiness, to be it, and to extend it outward to bless the world. As you do, you are initiating a spiritual propulsion more powerful than any worldly engine. And this generosity of the mystical mind reflects the fundamental nature of God. In reflecting God's love, we extend His love. And that which extends outward to bless others automatically extends inward as well. Your life will come to reflect your decision to use your mind for holy purposes.

Anything we do, anywhere we do it, is a chance to silently extend the blessing of our angelic spirit. We might be in line at the Department of Motor Vehicles—every person in line is someone we can bless. We might be waiting in a doctor's office—is there not someone waiting with us who could use a kind remark, or a child who would like us to read to them? As long as our hearts are open, we can show up fully as the angels we are. Imagine an angel saying to God, "Don't send me there, please. It's a boring town."

There is no corner of the earth in which God's love, expressed through you, is not desperately needed. And our most needed prayer, at times, is for the calming of our own impatient nature. We want an assignment from God, but we want it to be glamorous. However, if we look at our circumstances closely, we will usually see why they are perfect lessons for what we most need to learn, exactly as they are.

Often we want to jump out of a situation and into another, when we have not yet truly mastered the lessons inherent in the first one. Only when we have done that will our lives transform. Otherwise, no matter where we go or what we do, we will subconsciously manufacture the same situation over and over again.

Remember that Cinderella's godmother didn't "order out," but rather transformed the pumpkins and the mice and the rags that were already there. Anything and everything is the raw stuff of miracles. We don't have to be somewhere else, doing something else, to use our power to serve the holy and the good. Every single part of reality is an aspect of the greater glory of God.

Often, when the modern mind experiences itself as bored, it's actually merely addicted to cheap stimulation, having been trained by television and so forth to constantly jump out of its center. Learning how to slowly and purposefully arrange flowers in a vase, or how to enjoy ourselves while watching a small child play the same game over and over, can be a sign not of giving up but of growing up. We finally come to realize that there is not really a world out there at all, but merely a projection of all our private thought forms. Our capacity to behave powerfully in the outer world is increased by our ability to master the art of living serenely within the internal one.

And sometimes we are bored because the situation is asking us to do what we don't want to do, but would be better off if we did. When my child was very little, I lived in a small town for several years. While there, I didn't like it. I missed the action of a big city; I wanted the stimulation of late-night dinners at noisy restaurants. What other people considered calming and restful made me want to climb the walls.

And "just being a mother" felt boring to me at times. I found it difficult to be with my daughter the way she wanted me to. I would grow bored at the park, watching her slide down the same sliding board again and again or pushing her on the same swing for hours. Now I think it's the coolest thing in the world, being with a little child in the park, simply playing. I'm finally at a point where I can appreciate the beauty of just being somewhere; my nervous system no longer revolts against it. I am no longer under the illusion that there's more exciting action somewhere else.

What I realized—unfortunately, after I had left that town—was that my discomfort there was my detoxing from the overstimulation of the previous few years of my life. And the fact that I had very little to do while there besides being with my daughter was, in God's Mind, precisely the point! I had been given those four years as a gift: the divine opportunity to deeply and mindfully concentrate on bonding with my daughter. But because I was so agitated, emotionally resisting my circumstances, I was blind to many miracles that were offered to me. According to the Danish philosopher Søren Kierkegaard, "Life is lived forward but understood backward." The mystic seeks to deeply understand life while it's happening.

Today, my only desire is to make the most of whatever experiences I am having at the moment. And whenever I am tempted to think that those experiences are boring—that the excitement of life would surely lie somewhere else—then I remember that I am always at choice: experience the miracles of life as they come to me or blind myself to them, with the audacity to believe that God ever, ever, ever did not know what He was doing.

God *always* knows what He is doing—the question is, do we? The mystic, knowing there is nowhere where God is not, has realized His wisdom is unending. There is often hidden power in the times when nothing seems to be happening at all. The times when the material world takes less precedence are times when the holy has more chance to breathe. As I drive my daughter to school, we often use that time to pray for the day, to focus on what she would wish to have happen, and to surrender the day ahead to God. How could we consider it wasted time to have met with God and planned a new world?

4:00 pm

# Arguing

*"I should never have trusted you," he said,*
*gazing out the window and sipping his juice.*
*"You should never have trusted me?!" I jumped*
*to my feet. "Do you think this is my fault?"*
*"You should have called them on time."*
*"You should have paid the installment! I*
*couldn't call them when the bill wasn't paid!"*
*He looked at me with steely eyes.*
*No love, no humor.*
*I started to cry.*

Sometimes it's not the all-out wars, but the common arguments that wreck relationships. Love is strong, but it's also fragile. Everyone wants to be treated tenderly, and it's easy to forget that when we strongly disagree.

The mystic doesn't seek to avoid a disagreement so much as infuse it with grace. A disagreement is like a cut on the skin. You need to treat it gently and not cut further. So it should be, when we see things differently, that the gentleness of spirit guides our speech. Emotional havoc usually comes not from the issues that divide us so much as from the things we say and do because of the issues that divide us. Indeed, it's often fairly simple things that we disagree about. Learning how to disagree with love is an important skill on the mystical path.

First of all, we need to acknowledge that people do disagree. Avoiding a disagreement on the misguided principle that spiritual people don't have them is as spiritually immature as it is psychologically unsound. A disagreement and an argument are two different things. Indeed, a disagreement need not become an argument when the people involved have the personal skills to hold to higher consciousness while on lower ground.

According to *A Course in Miracles*, our job is to tell someone they're right, even when they're wrong. That doesn't mean we're supposed to lie. It does mean, however, that it's always our mission to affirm someone's humanity, even when we're disagreeing with his or her perceptions. Our spiritual challenge in any situation is first to recognize a person's love and innocence, and then to speak from that perspective. For it is not our disagreements that wound; it's our criticism, attack, and blame that wound. Until we know we're solidly on loving ground—past the temptation to even subtly blame— we had best be very careful with what we say and how we say it. Some words cut, while others heal.

But spirituality means a whole lot more than merely speaking in softer tones. Judgment can whisper, and it's still a judgment. Our spiritual task is to surrender the thought that we have the right, in any situation, to judge whom God would never judge, or to condemn whom God would never condemn. And that means everyone. God's perception is that each and every one of us is His beloved child in whom He is well pleased. And it is in learning to think as God thinks that we find mastery in life and love. So it is that when we disagree with someone, our prayer should not be that their eyes be opened to our point of view, but that our eyes be opened to theirs. According to *A Course in Miracles,* we try to understand someone in order to decide whether or not they're worthy of our love, but until we love them we cannot understand them.

Once we do—when we have allowed our hearts to soften into genuinely right relationship—the words with which we express ourselves in a disagreement become guided by a higher source. We remember to point out how much we appreciate someone before we point out what we perceive to be a problem. We are willing to express ourselves from a place of questioning rather than a place of blame. And we are able to see the difference between criticism, which tears people down, and honest disagreement, which can be a creative and even collaborative process.

When our basic humanity is affirmed, it's usually not that hard to hear people say that they disagree with us. Sometimes it's even fun, like a mental fencing match. But no one wants to feel the sword in their side. And anyone who places it there has not learned the spiritual skills of communication.

The problem, of course, is that it's not always easy to see the innocence in someone, particularly when we disagree with him or her. Yet that work—the inner effort to achieve our own right-mindedness—is the work that God requires of us. He does not need us to police the universe. He did not send us to Earth to set other people straight. He sent us here to become perfect ourselves, which we're not doing by definition when we are pointing our finger at someone else.

And the truth is, it doesn't feel good to separate ourselves from others through judgment or blame. It behooves us to ask ourselves, as it says in *A Course in Miracles,* "Do I prefer to be right or to be happy?"

When we disagree with someone, as much as we might be tempted to immediately express ourselves to them or to someone else about them, our best move is always to talk to God first. "Dear God, please take away my temptation to judge. Please show me this person as You would see them. Please show me their innocence, that I might see mine. Amen."

And then it is wise to hold our tongue until the hand of God has come upon us, readjusting our mental and emotional energies. The Holy Spirit needs time to work, like any kind of medicine, as it enters our psychic bloodstream. And when He does, He quickens the spirit within us. When that has occurred—when we are reconciled with our own divinity—we are automatically reconciled with others.

But until we are, we argue, and emotional danger looms. A small argument festers, and things are left unsaid. During the next encounter, someone makes a jab that is actually in reaction to what occurred before, and on and on, until grace breaks the chain. Finally, someone—and it need not be both parties—prays for help. "Dear God, please help us find the love between us. I know it's there, and I am willing to change, that I might see it. Thank you, God. Amen."

Listening to the ego—for whom separation is not a problem but a goal—we allow mental conflicts to separate our hearts. This divides us not only from one another, but also from the experience of God. For that place, where we feel we have been cast out of someone's heart, is our exile from the Garden of Eden. And in that exile, we are terrified. We then subconsciously respond from our terror—not at having been disagreed with, but at having been cast from the garden of God's love.

At such a moment, when we have been attacked, the mystic's prayer is to feel from God the love that has been denied us by someone else. We pray for the ability to send love to someone who has withheld it from us, that we not contribute to a wheel of suffering between us. Whether we are attacking someone or being attacked, our correction comes from the hand of God. It is our willingness to see things differently—our willingness to see that innocence beyond the veil of someone's personality—that opens our hearts to receive God's grace. And if that grace does not come immediately, that doesn't mean it isn't coming. There are layers of pain that we must burn through before we can recognize love in every situation. None of us can always do it, but our willingness confers upon us a mantle of light, and the light will penetrate the darkness of guilt. This penetration of darkness by the Light of God is a miracle in our hearts, and we will feel it when it comes.

Everything should be interpreted as love or as a call for love. When someone has not shown us their love, our power lies in knowing that they would have, had they known how. They are not wrong so much as they are wounded, and our role is not to judge them but to heal them. It is in cleaving to our own love that we awaken it in others.

In any situation where love does not rule, affirm that only love is real. Say it, repeat it, chant it like a mantra. Allow it to cast out all thoughts of blame and judgment and fear. Think of the mean-spiritedness of someone, then affirm that only love is real. Watch a horrible story on the TV news, then affirm that only love is real. Feel your own fears about this or that, then affirm that only love is real. This does not put you in a state of denial, but rather in a state of transcendence. You are not pretending that something is not really happening, but only that it is not Really happening. And just as the Wicked Witch of the West disappeared when Dorothy threw water on her, no manifestation of fear will long remain once humanity has risen to the understanding that only love is real.

If you've had a fight with someone, sit down and pray.

*Dear God, I surrender this argument to you.*
*Remove, Dear God, the walls between us.*
*Send your Spirit here to remind us both*
    *of our innocence and our love.*
*May forgiveness reign.*
*Dear God, may we begin again.*
*Amen.*

And think about how many times we've had arguments with friends or family that seemed so intense when they occurred, but years later, it's so easy to forgive because no one completely remembers anymore who said or did what to whom. We go through the years and we learn from life, finding it easier at last to both apologize and forgive. Ultimately, everything but love burns away. The power of forgiveness lies in knowing that will happen, even when it hasn't yet. We can skip the despair and go straight for the love. Instead of trying to find common ground, we can claim common ground. And, in fact, it is only the ground we stand on together that is even real at all.

# 5:00 pm

# Hoping Against Hope

*"He said when he left that he might be back—*
*that he needed some time to see this through—*
*then maybe he'd come back to us. I saw my*
*little boy cry but try to act like he wasn't,*
*when I told him that Dad wasn't coming*
*home tonight. The baby kept saying*
*"Daddy" softly, as I put her to bed.*
*And my oldest daughter said nothing.*
*If he doesn't come back, I don't know how*
*we'll live through this. Oh my God,*
*I hope he will. I hope he will. . . ."*

Sometimes we hope against hope for a particular outcome: our estranged spouse will come back, the cancer will be cured, we will get that job. Yet there are often times when we do not get that for which we most fervently wish. Not everyone who hopes for something gets it.

In the words of Dr. Martin Luther King, Jr., "If you lose hope, somehow you lose the vitality that keeps life moving; you lose that courage to be, that quality that helps you to go on in spite of all." But how do we retain the spirit of hope when our circumstances seem almost hopeless?

Hope springs eternal not because of the nature of the

world but because of the nature of God. The mystic knows that the light of Creation does not emanate from the material world, and so it is useless to seek it there. Nothing on the material plane is deeply stable. A house built on sand is vulnerable to weather, as Jesus said, while a house built on rock will stand. The material world is what the Buddha called *maya,* or illusion, testifying not to God's reality but to man's illusion of separation from God. It is not the true kingdom, and while it can *reflect* our good, it is a reflection only. It is not the *source* of our good because it is not the source of *us.*

It's best that we not place our hope in worldly satisfaction because, at the most fundamental level, there isn't any. Worldly satisfaction can bring temporary pleasure, which is certainly good. But nothing in the material world is deep enough to satisfy the true yearning of our souls. Our greatest hope is for the experience of joy, and often we are not as smart as we think we are when it comes to predicting what would bring us that joy. The mystic hopes not for a particular outcome, then, but for the *best* outcome for all concerned. And what that is can only be determined by God. Hope that is attached to a particular outcome is looking for pleasure but fishing for pain, because attachment itself is a source of pain. It is best to hope for an experience of life in all its fullness—a life that can embrace both joy and sorrow and still be at peace, because joy and sorrow are sure to come in this life. Our triumph over sorrow is not that we can avoid it but that we can endure it. And therein lies our hope, that in spirit we might become bigger than the problems we face.

Our problems in this world can surely be huge, but they are never as huge as God. The issue is never how bad things are, but *how good God is.* Hope lies in having more faith in the power of God to heal us than in the power of anything to hurt or destroy us. In realizing that as children of God we are bigger than our problems, we have the power at last to confront them. For all manifestation of fear is a reflection of the fact that humanity has forgotten its spiritual identity. In beginning to remember it, we put fear on notice that its days are numbered.

Where the ego analyzes a problem, the spirit accepts that there is an ultimate answer that is the Answer to every problem. And that is why we place what we hope for in the hands of God. Our hope is that He will illumine our hearts—that we will become the people He would have us be—for in the presence of an awakened spirit, all problems fall away.

We are the children of a loving God *for whom nothing is impossible.* As we remember that, we become as powerful as we are meant to be. We are not meant to cower before the darkness of the world; let it cower before *us*. Every problem is merely another opportunity to use the miraculous powers we've been given.

The suffering of the world is not the point of human existence; the point of human existence is that in God all suffering ends. Through God, we celebrate a happy ending to every situation, *convinced that it has already occurred*. And it's out of that conviction that miracles arise. The resurrection of Jesus, Buddha's enlightenment under the Bodhi tree, and the deliverance of the Israelites to the promised land are not fairy tales; they are messages from God. Their point is not what we should hope for, but rather what we should consider done, the miracles we can lean on because they were accomplished for all eternity. God has built into the structure of Creation that everything dark will turn light again.

True hope lies not in an illness cured or a marriage reconciled, but in a state of mind. The woman whose husband has left her should pray not that he come home, but that God carry her through this ordeal even if he doesn't. She should not pray, "Dear God, please make my husband come back to me," for she knows that God has given us all free will. But she prays, in spite of her tears, "Dear God, I place this situation in your hands. May my husband find true happiness; may we all find true happiness. If his happiness lies here with me, then please touch his heart. And if it does not, then please heal mine. May Your will be done. Amen."

The resurrective tendency of the universe is always at work in our personal trials and in our collective challenges. God, in His awesomeness and infinitude, has provided a solution to every problem the moment the problem occurs. The part that any of us can play in providing that solution is etched on our hearts. Even now, while the world is suffering the scourge of terror, our faith is to remember that God's harmony reigns supreme. God's light is not always our experience, but it can always be our faith. "Blessed are those who have faith who cannot see." For someone who is in prison, true hope lies not simply in an early release date, but in the knowledge that in God's world, there are no walls. The only walls that can hold us back are the walls that divide our hearts. Even within prison walls, we can cultivate a heavenly garden by fostering a beloved community. Our hope in God is not a hope for something to happen in the world, but for something to happen in us.

Essentially, our greatest hope has already been realized. Heaven is here and now, in our capacity to realize our oneness. Nothing can happen to make God not God, love not the only reality, or spirit not eternal. Our hope has already been met with a gigantic "yes" from God. *We* are the ones who keep saying no.

Still, the offer to love instead of fear remains. We can choose again, at any moment. We can withdraw our faith in the thought forms that have guided us to where we are, realizing their complete inadequacy to guide us where we would like to go. To place our hope in God is to place our hope in love. We're not hoping that this or that will happen, but that we'll achieve a state of consciousness in which, whatever happens, we will not swerve from love or peace. Hope is simply an attitude, placing trust in the mystery of the universe before trust in the things of this world.

God has promised our return to the garden, but when we get there is entirely up to us. We may travel long and vicious lengths down the paths of fear. But someday, somewhere, we realize that our choice is either to live in fear or to learn to live another way. God is not our servant, but our deliverer. He enters where we invite Him, but an invitation not offered in love is not an invitation at all. Our hope is that, one day, He will have taught us how to love one another so completely that our world will become His garden.

In the meantime, our hope is born of participation in hopeful solutions, for, ultimately, the only way to feel hope is to give hope to someone else. And then we see that it is all around us. The world should feel hopeful because *you* are here. You *are* the hope, because God is in you.

# 6:00 pm

# Feeling Guilty

*I was driving home three blocks. The*
*stop sign was there—I had seen it*
*before—but that day I was in a hurry.*
*I don't remember hitting the car, but I*
*remember seeing it fly across the intersection.*
*I saw the car doors open and children started*
*piling out, several of them, more than I would*
*have thought possible for one car. . . .*
*And then came the woman, holding a baby.*
*I had no idea whether or not the child was*
*alive. The woman looked at me and said,*
*so soulfully, "Why, Lady, why?"*

Sometimes we feel we've made a mess of something important, and it seems there is nothing we can do to change it. We look back with remorse and wish to ourselves, "If only I had said this," or, "If only I had done that." We can spend years condemning ourselves for having failed to realize the wisdom of a course we chose not to take or the ridiculousness of one we did.

At such times we're apt to ask ourselves, "What could I have been *thinking*?" Yet often we find that the problem was not what we were thinking, but *that we were not really thinking at all*. We were not deeply reflective, much less spiritu-

ally guided, in making a particular decision. We simply surrendered to the shallow thoughts that too often pass for real
thinking today, following the path of least resistance (often
the path of least nobility, virtue, and conscience). And now
we are suffering accordingly.

Fortunately, from a metaphysical perspective, the past
can always be reclaimed. In the words of *A Course in Miracles,*
"Nothing can be lost except in time, and time does not exist."
Even if we've chosen a path that was not illumined, one that
was not an expression of love or wisdom, then the possibility we chose not to manifest *still exists* as an abstract reality.
It is like a computer file that exists but has not been downloaded. The loving reaction to any situation—regardless
whether or not it has been manifest—dwells as a possibility
in the mind of God, and therefore awaits our decision to
choose it.

Let's say Jennifer was unkind to you. She betrayed a
confidence or lied about you to a coworker, though now
she has apologized. You might not have been forgiving toward her, though that certainly would have been the highest expression of your essential self. You might have
understood the need for forgiveness, perhaps, but it was
still too much of a stretch for you emotionally. The fact that
you *might* have forgiven her—that in an enlightened state

you *would* have forgiven her—means that the choice for forgiveness will be waiting for you until you're ready. You will now meet Jennifer, or someone just like her, no matter where you go. For forgiving the particular issue she represents in your life is the lesson your soul needs to learn. That issue will now be scripted into the curriculum of your life's journey, to motivate you to find your true self, your loving self that is aligned with the forgiveness of God. You will become more careful with your confidences and also less sensitive to other people's opinions. After encountering an issue and getting it wrong a few times, we become much more motivated to get it right. Praying for Jennifer, sending her light and love, is a mystical practice with far more power than anything the ego would have us do. It is the only thing that will make us invulnerable to the lovelessness of others.

In any given moment, with everything we think or say or do, it's as though we're pushing a button on a computer and bringing up a particular file. There is an infinite number of files in the universe, and one of them is named "God's Will." We click on this file by praying, "May God's will be done." Life is so much easier when we live by that thought, for it is a prayer for right-mindedness. It is a prayer that we create only the good. We might choose a file other than "God's Will"—let's say "Defensiveness," "Blame," or "Control"—but the file marked "God's Will" still exists in the computer and can be downloaded at another time. It's the one file that can never, ever be deleted from the system.

You made a lot of money, but you weren't ready to stop self-sabotaging? You had a wonderful partner, but you failed to realize how lucky you were? You had wonderful kids, but you spent too little time with them and now you hardly know them? There are so many ways that a person can blow it. And while our guilt can sometimes feel overwhelming, remember there is nothing that God cannot do. There is no gap He cannot fill. There is no mistake too big for God to rectify.

Feeling guilty serves no one, but rather keeps us stuck in self-defeating patterns. Humility lies in atoning for our errors—becoming fully accountable for them in our own minds, and if necessary in our communication with others—and asking God to heal us. Only then can we begin again from a healed and holy place.

Whenever we have strayed from the light, thoughtlessly or recklessly plowing ahead without God's guidance, we can always go back in our minds to the moment we made the mistake, humbly turn it over to God, and ask for the chance to begin again. The following prayer, from *A Course in Miracles,* is for just that moment. We are reminded by the Course, "The Holy Spirit will respond fully to your slightest invitation."

*I must have decided wrongly, because I am not at peace.*
*I made the decision myself, but I can also decide otherwise.*
*I want to decide otherwise, because I want to be at peace*
*I do not feel guilty, because the Holy Spirit will undo all the*
   *consequences of my wrong decision if I will let Him.*
*I choose to let Him, by allowing Him to decide for God*
   *for me.*

Once the pain of guilt begins to recede, the alchemical processes of transformation will begin. We can feel ourselves growing in spiritual maturity. Our thoughts and actions grow stronger and wiser. Through the grace of God, we become more spiritually aware in the area in which we made the mistake than we were even before we made it. When we have forgiven ourselves—"Yep, I'm a human being and I make mistakes!"—and made appropriate amends, then God's spirit will offer us another chance at the fullness of life and love. Sometimes it's the same situation brought back around again, and we will be grateful in ways we were not grateful before, never again taking the miracles of life for granted. The next time we meet Jennifer on the road, there will be no need to experience anything but peace with her.

In our youth, we are tempted to think that nothing really matters. We have so much time, it doesn't matter; so much love, it doesn't matter; and so much of everything, it doesn't matter. But when we've lived enough—and made enough mistakes—we learn how very much things matter. We're often horrified at how carelessly we had lived before.

Yet God's compassion is with us at every step, not seeking to judge but to heal, that we might learn from life and then proceed differently. We've usually not done as much damage as we fear, and God is so infinitely powerful that He can transform and redeem whatever damage we did do. It is part of the miraculous mercy of God that He is there for us when we've made a mistake, as much as He is there for us when we've been our very best.

In the Bible, it was the returning Prodigal Son who received a great reception from his father, while the son who had not left home received no such fanfare. And we are an entire generation of Prodigal Sons. Our false ambitions, our idolatry, our breaches of integrity, our lack of ethics, our societal injustices—there is something for almost any conscious person to feel guilty about, for who among us has not been tainted by the corruptions of our time? But it is the darkest places that lead us to light when they lead us to the arms of God. Such is the infinite nature of His love, that there is nothing we can do to make Him turn His back on us, though we so often turn our backs on Him. To punish ourselves endlessly for our mistakes is to doubt His mercy. Do we need to make amends? Yes. Do we need to "take a fearless moral inventory," being honest about our weaknesses and willing to let them go? Absolutely. But do we need to go live forever with the guilty feelings of a hopeless sinner? No, because the meaning of sin is that we missed the mark—we made a mistake. And God's desire is always to heal us, not punish us; to correct our thinking, not make us pay.

The mistakes I've made in my life have humbled me, helping me to become a person who may or may not have the same chances again to do the wonderful things I might have done before. But I know that the person I am today, honed in some way by the hours of remorse I've experienced, is better prepared to face the future. My mistakes have been my teachers, and my only job is to learn from them.

Sometimes the past is so painful to think about that your only salvation lies in complete surrender to the mercy of God. Only in Him are you given the strength and courage it takes to keep on walking when every step is hard. But, finally, after what can seem like an endless journey into the darkness of your own regret, you come upon the light again. You have no doubt who has set you free, for only One who is the author of forgiveness would give you still another chance.

*Dear God,*
*Please take the past from me.*
*I did \_\_\_\_, which I regret.*
*I go back to that moment*
*And I give it to You.*
*Please, dear God,*
*Make right my wrongs*
*And take away my sorrow.*
*Forgive me, please.*
*May I begin again.*
*Amen.*

# 7:00 pm

# Grieving

*She was a third-grade teacher and she just
kept working, through chemo and radiation
and numerous hospital stays. For more than
four years, she was such a trooper. But when
her boss could no longer take the sight of
her head scarf, she took away her classroom
and broke my sister's heart. It was that—
not the cancer—that killed her.
When she lost her breast, she could take
the pain. But when she lost her
classroom, she was done. . . .*

Four or five days before my sister died of cancer, my brother and I sat with her in her bedroom. She was sitting up in bed, surrounded by the kind of halo-like aura that I have often seen around those who are nearing death. My brother and I were emotional, but my sister had already passed into that almost weird serenity that often accompanies one's final hours. I began to cry, saying through my tears that the three of us hadn't taken full advantage of the opportunity we'd been given to experience what it really meant to be siblings. We hadn't spent enough time together; we had kvetched about each other as often as we had celebrated each other; we had loved each other, but passively, with sniping and complaining often drowning out our deeper feelings. And now I saw that we had utterly failed to embrace the miracle of our love for one another. In fact, we had had no idea that it *was* a miracle. My brother sadly nodded in agreement. But my sister said, "Yes, but it's okay, because we get it now."

And there, in that moment, we really did. All three of us did. We experienced a depth of connection that we had never known, between and among us, our entire lives. Yet the fact that we had experienced even that glimpse of genuine oneness proved that such a state is possible. Whenever I think of humanity's destiny, I think of that moment with my brother and sister, and I know in my heart where we are *meant* to be going. We're meant for that shimmering, radiant place where everything except what is most deeply true has melted away, and we can truly see.

We should not have to be at death's threshold to realize that everything but love is unimportant. Yet often it's the things that are most sad that remind us how much we have to be happy about. Tears of sorrow often pave the way for tears of joy. I will never take a relationship for granted again, the way I took for granted my relationship with my sister. For the rest of my life, I will try to squeeze every last bit of juice out of love. Losing a love that mattered to me taught me to love in a way I never would have known.

And I don't just grieve that I didn't know my sister longer; I grieve that I didn't know her *better.* Often we grieve most bitterly over things we had but did not allow ourselves fully to experience. Whatever is lived fully is easier to let go.

Tears have taught me a tremendous amount, and I know now that they often come bearing important gifts. There has emerged a half-baked spiritual myth that invalidates sadness, claiming it is beneath us if we are walking the path to true enlightenment. But surely one of the most powerful lines in the Bible is one of the simplest: "Jesus wept." There is nothing unenlightened about crying over the tragedy of human suffering; perhaps what is neurotic is how infrequently we do. There is an old Buddhist story about a monk who stood crying at the grave of his master. A traveler came by and saw his tears. "Why would you cry? I thought you were enlightened!" The monk replied, "Because I am sad."

Our task is not to avoid painful emotion, but rather to transform it at its roots. And that we cannot do if we don't go through the emotion authentically. Sadness has to be experienced in order to be transcended. No situation can be transformed until it is accepted as it is.

Remember that when her stepmother and stepsisters

drove away to the ball, Cinderella simply sat down and cried. They had quite literally left her in the dust, headed for all things fabulous while she had to stay at home. Surely Cinderella would have been justified had she run after their carriage shouting obscenities. But she didn't do that, for she is a being on the way to genuine awakening. Getting angry would not have helped, running after her stepmother and stepsisters would not have helped, and scheming to punish them would not have helped. Such behavior might have satisfied her ego but not her soul. Cinderella, in tune with her emotional and spiritual essence, simply sat down and allowed herself to cry.

Cinderella was true to her feelings, remaining in grief as opposed to resisting the pain of it. She surrendered not to anger but to tears. And in that state of pure sorrow at having suffered so deeply the cruelty of the world, she magnetized the presence of a divine, illumined being. There is a direct connection between Cinderella's emotional integrity and her fairy godmother's appearance. By aligning herself with a higher truth, Cinderella automatically called down the inspired intercession of otherworldly forces.

The key to finding the miracle inside sadness lies in learning how to allow ourselves to *be* sad. This is often harder than one would think. We live in a culture that mitigates genuine emotion of any kind, because it mitigates genuine *anything.* In a culture of denial, those who do not deny the depths of their feelings are often branded as fools or hysterics. Emotion not manipulated specifically for the purposes of selling something is seen as having little intrinsic value. Crying is often viewed as a waste of time or a sign of weakness. We no longer give deep cultural permission for the processes of grief; after all, it's an inconvenience to the speedy wheels of the status quo. Are you sad? Deal with it. Take this pill. Process it. And hurry. Someone once said to a friend of mine, "Your mother's been dead a month already! Aren't you over it yet?"

But grief that is suppressed will force its way to expression—whether we want it to or not. It often emerges in dysfunctional ways when not allowed its proper place in the psychic and social scheme of things. There was a time when widows wore widow's weeds for a year, as past societies had a more sophisticated understanding of sadness and grief. They knew that both must be *allowed* in order for life to go on. The modern idea that we should move quickly through grief—because for some insane reason we should move quickly through *everything*—ensures that we will never move through anything in a very deep way. And then life actually does not go on at all, so much as it continually repeats itself.

So it is that the modern mystic, when experiencing the heartbreak of life, does not avoid the heartbreak nor try to distance from it in the name of spirituality, mental health, or anything else. Enlightenment does not consist of pretending to be where we are not; enlightenment means being in touch with where we are and being willing to learn what God would have us learn from it. Sometimes the purpose of a day is to merely feel our sadness, knowing that as we do we allow whole layers of grief, like old skin cells, to drop off us.

The wisdom that comes from having experienced heartbreak cannot be bequeathed; it can only be gained through experience. And having truly felt it, we are far more likely to have compassion for others. Anything that takes us closer to true compassion takes us closer to what will one day be an experience of even greater joy.

Life is often cruel. Yet I have found that there is a grief that is infused with the grace of God. At my sister's funeral, as I wept uncontrollably, my father, age eighty-five and nearing the end of his own life, leaned over to me, put his arms around me, and said, "Littlest Sister, it's all a part of the mystery." He was there, in the place where he could see that. I could see it in his eyes. And as I leaned my head upon his shoulder, continuing to cry, I knew I was on my way to the place where I would see it, too.

# 8:00 pm

# Learning Compassion

*My sister was teaching severely disturbed children, and one day I went to assist her with her class. I met a little boy I will never forget, because it was as though he was a boy but he was not a boy. He did not seem fully human. As I tried to keep him from attacking a box of M&M's like an animal, I realized I was trying to reason with someone who wasn't there.*

*Completely shaken, I ran into the bathroom, crying. In a few minutes' time, my sister followed me. "What are you doing?!" she scolded. "Get back in there!"*

*"I can't stand it!" I cried. "It's too hard! It's so sad!"*

*"Get back in there!" she commanded. "He doesn't need your pity! He needs your help!"*

One of the things I often wonder about is how I got so lucky. I constantly read about people whose lives are so much harder than mine. On one hand, I don't believe in luck; on the other hand, I'm certainly clear that living as a woman in a democratic society is a lot more fortunate than, let's say, living as a woman in Afghanistan under the Taliban. I have known sadness and grief, of course. But some people—far too many people—live lives of unending suffering, through no fault of their own. From children dying of AIDS in Africa, to young Israelis and Palestinians whose lives are put in danger by a hatred they did nothing to cause, to peo-

ple in India and elsewhere living under conditions of crush-
ing poverty, to people in our own country who are incar-
cerated unjustly—what is the mysterious force that seems to
assign to some people such misery and to others such abundance and ease?

While many religions claim to answer that question, the
fact remains that there are things we cannot know. Whatever
is happening is simply happening. And, from a spiritual perspective, anything negative that happens has only one purpose: to foster compassion in the human heart. Anything
can fuel the fires of compassion if our hearts are open wide
enough. As it is written in the Bible, "What man has intended for evil, God intends for good." Even the most hor-
rific situations can increase within us our capacity to love.

I have actually heard people say, about children dying of
hunger or people living in war-torn regions, "Well, that is
their karma"—as though that somehow ends the conversation. What an astounding way to avoid the responsibility of
bearing witness to human suffering. The night before he was
crucified, Jesus sat awake in the garden of Gethsemane.
When his disciples began to fall asleep around him, he said
to them, "What, can you not watch with me one hour?" Even
when there is nothing we specifically can do to help our suffering neighbor, there is spiritual power in remaining awake
with someone in the hour of his or her agony. In bearing wit-

ness to human suffering, we light a candle in the dark that illumines the most painful night.

Just as some people have talent for art, and others for science, some seem to have a greater talent for compassion. Examples abound of humanitarian workers risking their lives for people living the ravages of war, of doctors giving of their talents and abilities to help those in poverty-stricken societies. But not every act of compassion is dramatic. All of us in our own way, just by being more tender and loving, can open our hearts and make a difference in someone's life. Compassion is not just emotion; it is *force*. It is an aspect of the infinite power of God. Humanity's next great leap in consciousness will be the realization that love is a *power to be applied*—no less than the power of steam, the power of electricity, or the power of the atom.

What if all of us dedicated ourselves to efforts of compassion for people we will never even know, and who will probably never know us? What an extraordinary burst of light would pervade the world, should a shift in consciousness from narcissism to compassion become a common miracle among us. At what point does the heart burst open and commit itself to doing something, *anything,* if it will possibly make a difference in easing the pain of someone else?

There were ages when people sat on great powers, yet did not know how to harness them for practical purposes. We knew there was an atom long before we knew how to split it. People enjoyed the beauty of Niagara Falls long before its hydroelectric power lit whole cities. Today, we know there is love in our hearts, but we have only begun to scratch the surface of how we can use it to restore and transform our world. It is the task of our generation to turn love into a social *force*. The most significant development of the twenty-first century will be the harnessing of the social potential of love.

Most of us don't lack compassion so much as we *avoid* it. We resist compassion in the United States with a peculiar hypocrisy, extolling the virtues of volunteerism, for instance, while making volunteerism more of a necessity by diminishing our budgetary commitments to the poor and powerless. We take away housing for thousands, then build a hundred houses for Habitat for Humanity and everyone gets to feel good. Our primary response to human suffering appears to be making sure it occurs on the other side of town or the other side of the world.

In the Buddhist religion, the search for God is synonymous with the realization of our most compassionate self. The Buddha, like Jesus, lived a life that personified the path to divine Selfhood. The Buddha was born a wealthy prince named Siddhartha, whose father wished to protect him from the cruelty and the suffering of life. To this end, he built walls around his palace, only allowing in the pleasures of the material world. But the young Siddhartha instinctively knew that there was more to life than what he saw within the confines of his father's palace, and *he also knew he needed to experience those things in order to become truly human.* He left behind his beautiful wife and child, journeying beyond the walls of the palace to encounter human suffering for the first time. And, with that, his journey to enlightenment began.

Ultimately, the Buddha would reveal that untransformed human life *is* suffering, and out of that revelation would come enlightenment for millions. From his recognition that the palace walls we build around ourselves are merely holding the truth and meaning of human existence at bay came his exhortation to recognize the suffering of the world. We must open our hearts before suffering, he claimed, in order to become genuine channels for its transcendence. We live in a prison—not a palace—when our hearts have not yet cracked open.

But when the heart does crack open—when humanity's pain and suffering moves us to respond to it as passionately as we used to run away from it—then we are on our way to enlightenment at last. We realize our oneness with the angels, as we offer ourselves to help them. Every time we say a prayer for someone, serve a meal to a homebound person with AIDS, hold the hand of a dying patient as a hospice volunteer, give a deserving, struggling employee another chance to get it right, or lobby our elected officials for more compassionate policies, we are tending to our own evolution.

That which purports to be spiritual growth but does not involve an active compassion is not really growth at all. Whether we are seeking to heal ourselves or our planet, we must commit acts of compassion that go beyond the individual, beyond what is convenient, and beyond the confines of the status quo. Individual acts of kindness and compassion will not of themselves provide enough loving energy to transform our civilization. Rather, we must make love the center of all our enterprises—collective, as well as individual. When harmlessness toward life becomes a personal, social, economic, and political imperative, we will be on our way at last to the restoration and regeneration of our civilization.

We have an opportunity at this time in history to completely change the course of human culture. That opportunity is not simply an option anymore, it is a gauntlet thrown down by the forces of history, before a generation still not yet decided whether money and power or love and brotherhood should form the basis of our civilization. And we will decide, or life will decide for us. The human species *will* learn to become profoundly compassionate toward itself and toward all life. We will learn it through wisdom, or we will learn it through pain. But we will learn, because it's God's will that we become the people He has created us to be. It's not up to us where we are going—but how we get there, and when, is determined by every choice we make, every moment of every day.

# PART III

# A Life of Grace

# Ritual

During the twentieth century, the Western mind fell into a materialistic stupor, so enamored of visible, tangible complexities that invisible realities were shoved to the margins of our consciousness and our culture. Scientific truths were deemed real in an unassailable way, while spiritual truths were often thought to be superstitious relics of an age gone by.

Fortunately, the pendulum always swings back, and at last we are emerging from the rationalistic fog of an over-secularized worldview. We are collectively remembering that we are spiritual beings, the remembrance itself like Atlantis rising from a sea of ancient forgetfulness. It arises new, trans-formed, and cleansed of what it used to stand for, now rec-ognized as key to both our mission and our joy. The material world can be a marvelous place, full of power and excite-ment, but it is not—even in its most intense manifestations—the world of ultimate truth. Only the truth of a radical, fundamental love is unalterable and eternal. Our own will may delay its expression, but love will always prevail. It's the truth we remember at the end of our lives, or perhaps at the end of the life of a loved one. It's the truth we see when the superficial preoccupations that compete for our attention and rob us of our life force begin at last to melt away.

This truth is reaffirmed by our participation in holy rit-ual. A sacred ceremony casts a spell on our hearts. It re-minds us who we are, thus releasing us to become who we are capable of being. Rituals provide points of genuine con-nection with what is most authentically true—in ourselves, in each other, and in God. They are portals to divine radi-ance, and the light we receive through them remains with us.

Sacred ritual illuminates the meaning with which we have imbued a human experience, raising it to the realm of the divine. And it is in those places where we are most pro-foundly human that we are pregnant with divine possibilities: It's deeply human to give birth to a child, to grow into ado-lescence, to marry, to mature into our elder years, and to die. It's not an accident that traditional religious ceremonies take place in these moments; it's when we are most fully and vulnerably alive that our hearts cry out for an added dimension of soulfulness. It is when we are deeply touched by life that we most want to feel God's touch upon us. Holy ceremony marries the mortal and the immortal—the secular and the sacred—that from that point forward, the two shall be irrevocably connected within us.

When I was a child, I had a sense, as most children do, of the mysterious power of religious ritual. I loved being in synagogue, going to weddings, going to Bar Mitzvahs. I could feel the mystical energies they aroused within me. But as I grew older, I learned to forget the subtle vibrations of spiritual energy that emanate from moments of religious depth. Weddings became about bridal registries and pretty dresses, and baptisms became about baby gifts. I was not a child of God anymore so much as a child of American culture. The world we live in is too much with us; materialism bombards us relentlessly, and we surrender to its dominance at a terrible price. Consciousness attunes itself to one realm or another: We either vibrate with the world or we vibrate with spirit, and one casts out the other.

The mind cannot serve two masters, and according to *A Course in Miracles,* we can be either "host to God or hostage to the ego." A mystic has made a choice for love, more than willing to sacrifice a materialistic perspective for a far richer, more varied, and more harmonious picture. That doesn't mean, of course, that baby gifts are not important or that brides shouldn't get the right serving forks. It doesn't mean we shouldn't live in lovely houses or enjoy beautiful things. It simply means that a mystical worldview puts the world in perspective, with eternal things in first place and everything else in second place. A fancy wedding does not guarantee marital bliss, no matter how beautiful it is. But a genuinely sacred marriage ceremony—be it Christian, Jewish, Muslim, Hindu, or our own spiritual hybrid—has the spiritual power to weave two hearts together.

When I was growing up, so many traditional rituals had become empty shells, performed perfunctorily by bored and boring officiants, with little power to genuinely uplift the spirit. In many cases my generation rejected them, seeking more modern relevance. Yet often we threw away the baby with the bathwater, desacralizing our sacraments in an effort to be more authentic, more "real." What we failed to real-ize is that the substance of sacred ritual is forever new and forever relevant. The problem, when there is one, lies not in rituals; the problem lies in the consciousness of those who perform them.

Rituals become empty when imbued with empty

thoughts. Those who overemphasize the external world don't know how to *meet* ritual, to imbue it with the kind of meaning that emanates from a heart truly open and vulnerable before God. Today, people are recognizing anew that rituals can create cellular shifts within us. If someone commits in a sacred ceremony to the care and protection of another— whether as parent, godparent, or mate—then that commitment carries a spiritual, emotional weight that no legal transaction can ever match. Rituals evoke a commitment of the heart. When the shadow of the hand of God has come over us, lifting us to new purpose or binding our heart to someone else's, bringing comfort when a loved one has died or calling us to new magnificence and power, we know it. The Holy Spirit is not metaphor or symbol; it is a living, alchemical power that infuses our hearts with the glory of God.

I don't hear many people say anymore, "Why get married? It's just a piece of paper." For marriage, when placed within a sacred context, is not just a piece of paper. And more people today seem to realize that yes, you do go to the funeral, because it does make a difference. Prayers for the dead and prayers for their loved ones left on this earth create a field of blessing that is palpable, that is felt. It is not for nothing that the Holy Spirit is called "the Comforter." We are emotionally healed as we allow ourselves to surrender to the sanctity of a spirit-filled ceremony. We feel our souls have been bathed in light.

Many people, who might not have ever thought about it before, now want their babies blessed, and their adolescents to experience meaningful rituals marking this new stage of their lives. People are rediscovering the power of ritual both in traditional and nontraditional ways. We embrace rites of passage for adolescents and elders; we take vision quests and attend Native American sweat lodges; we perform solstice rituals and healing ceremonies for the Earth; we create birthday ceremonies and sacred New Year's Eve services, in which we surrender to God the disharmony of the year passing and ask for blessing on the year being born.

As an officiant, I have found that what people want from rituals is not that they be fancy, but that they be genuine. We do not need the specific words of a prewritten text so much as we need authenticity before God; we do not need an ordained officiant to perform our ritual so much as we need a spirit-filled consciousness; and we do not need external glamour, but rather internal simplicity before the throne of God.

As we participate in the miraculous process of holy ritual, we feel ourselves expand into the space of a mythical reality. In a coming-of-age ceremony, a mother named Carol is no longer just Carol bowing before her daughter Danielle as the young girl reaches puberty: She is every woman, honoring the emergence of every girl into adulthood. And from that point forward, Carol will not be the same, for something within her will have been altered. She has entered through a door that marks a greater fullness of her womanhood as mother, elder, and mentor to all young women. And Danielle will have been altered as well, as she is no longer a young girl, but is now rather a young woman. This will affect her relationship to herself, to others, and to everything around her. Her pysche will rearrange itself as her body already has.

The spirit needs constant care and nourishment, just like the body. And it is a process that must go on continually. For ages, religious ritual has been used as preventative medicine, keeping our lives infused with light that we might be less vulnerable to darkness. In this country, we're very good about praying once tragedy has struck. But if we prayed together more often, so much tragedy might not occur! A sacred ritual—even something as simple as lighting a prayer candle every morning—can make a tremendous difference in the quality of our lives.

From the oracles of Delphi to the Passover seder, from Midnight Mass on Christmas Eve to the beginning prayers of Ramadan, from chants on Buddha's birthday to the celebration of Krishna's triumphant presence, there are so many ways to elevate our relationship with God to the highest heights. We commune with Him, pour out our hearts to Him, receive Him, and are touched by Him. To the devoted heart, these are not just words. Whether saying a blessing or burying the dead, the moments when we reach out to God are the moments when our lives are graced with light.

Every time a flower blossoms, God demonstrates His grace. Every time a snowflake forms, God demonstrates His grace. Every time spring comes around again, God demonstrates His grace. Every time a baby is born, God demonstrates His grace. And every time someone takes their final breath, God demonstrates His grace as well.

We cannot match God's handiwork, but we can mirror His holiness. In every sacred ritual, we show Him our love and He shows us His. We are reminded of the constant presence of an all-loving, all-giving, all-merciful God. A holy ceremony is an act of spiritual intimacy, in which we connect deeply to our divine source. Having touched, however faintly, the Mind of God, our minds and even our bodies are blessed.

Having received a blessing of our deep humanity, we realize finally that we are more than human. We are creatures of fertile earth and endless sky, meant to embody their full integration. We are floating in the waters of an amniotic spirit, within a cosmic womb out of which we will emerge angelic and joyful. Praise and thanks and music and tears transform us. The time has come for us to be reborn.

The sacred moments of holy ritual are fragile and gentle, yet more powerful than the sea. And within the waters of that holy sea, we grow as our ancient ancestors grew. As they left the sea and climbed onto land, we reach beyond the land to find our wings and fly. In time, we shall soar through the mystical skies as easily as we now walk on land.

And life itself will be one long moment of gentle, unbroken grace.

# Sabbath

The Fourth Commandment is "Observe the Sabbath and keep it holy." It's amazing, if you think about it, that observing the Sabbath is right up there with "Thou shalt not steal" and "Thou shalt not kill." Why is it so important to God that we take one day out of every week and surrender it to Him?

The wording in the Bible is, "Remember the Sabbath day, to keep it holy. Six days shalt thou labor, and do all thy work; but the seventh day is the Sabbath of the Lord thy God. . . . For in six days the Lord made heaven and earth, the sea, and all that in them is, and rested the seventh day;

wherefore the Lord blessed the Sabbath day, and hallowed it."
The Sabbath would be *His* day.

Having a relationship with God is in many ways like having a relationship with anyone else. In order for it to blossom, we must make time for it and tend to it with genuine
attention. Observing the Sabbath is like having a steady date
with God, setting aside time in our calendar of days to dedicate to our connection with Him. And in remembering who
God is, we remember who we are. Knowing ourselves
clearly in relationship to God, we are stronger in our relationship with everyone and everything.

As the leader of an interfaith spiritual fellowship, I have
experienced the metaphysical power of a Sabbath service.
For a Sabbath service is more than just bodies gathered in a
room: It is a convening of hearts and minds in an internal as
well as external sanctuary. The mind is our true altar and the
heart our true sanctuary from the cruelty and limitations of
the world. In Sabbath fellowship, we enter with others into
the Inner Room. We go there to remember God, worship
Him, and recommit our hearts to Him. We experience the
stereophonic effect of amplified prayer emanating from the
hearts of many. We participate in the creation of a devo-
tional field of energy, which blesses its participants and remains with us when we leave the service.

Like taking a trip to a chiropractor's office to have our

spine realigned, we attend a Sabbath service to have our mind and heart realigned. The power of God is not outside us but inside, and when the mind and heart are aligned with His spirit, then His will is accomplished within and without. Outside the blessing of that divine alignment, we are vulnerable to the machinations of the ego mind, where fear and chaos rule.

The Sabbath is a day when the ego takes a rest. We keep our minds on God's love—both His love for us and the love He would have us share with each other. And that strengthens us in ways that nothing else can do. Just as we recharge a computer or a cell phone, on the Sabbath we recharge our souls. Day in and day out, most of us are preoccupied with essentially meaningless things. We know this grind is not in keeping with our heart's deepest desire, yet we often feel trapped by our ego's demands. Our lives revolve around concerns that do not resonate with the grandeur of our spiritual identity, and yet, unchecked, those concerns devour our energy and time. The purpose of the Sabbath is to interrupt this pattern of superficial preoccupations and return our minds to a path of holiness and peace. It is a day we invest in God in order to reinvest in ourselves.

There was a musical very popular in my childhood called *Stop the World! I Want to Get Off!* Sabbath is a day when we simply get off the worldly merry-go-round and remember the truth of who we are. We are placed on this earth to love away the pain of the world, yet we cannot do that when we ourselves are living at the effect of it.

I had not expected, when I first took a pulpit, that the experience of a Sabbath service would be so different from any other spiritual lecture. Yet, in a subtle way, it is. There's something about people joining together specifically for a worship service on a holy day that makes the effect of prayer and prayerfulness particularly potent. Jews don't have to go to synagogue on Friday or Saturday; Christians don't have to go to church on Sunday morning. But when we do, we join in an experience of fellowship not only with other worshipers, but in a way with people all over the world, that we might receive the spirit of a living God.

Like boxers who go back to a corner when the bell rings, to be attended to by handlers, on the Sabbath we go back to our own corner to be ministered to by angels. For angels are the thoughts of God. Sabbath is a day to remember His thoughts: to forgive ourselves and others; to reconcile ourselves with Him; to study more deeply the principles of Truth; to pray for blessing and protection in the days ahead; and, most of all, to commune with the miraculous spirit of true life, as opposed to the spirit of shallowness and illusion that is in fact a living death.

One Sunday morning, when conflict in the Middle East

was at a particularly high and violent point, I chose as the topic for my Sunday sharing: "How we might spiritually help create peace between Israel and the Palestinians." I asked if anyone in the audience was a native Palestinian or an Arab who felt strongly about the Palestinian cause. A man put his hand up. I asked if anyone in the audience was a native Israeli, or a Jew who felt strongly about Israel. A woman put her hand up. Then I asked both of them if they would be willing to participate in a healing ceremony. What followed was a prayerful apology, both by a Palestinian, on behalf of his people, for all violence and transgressions perpetrated against Israel and Israelis; and an apology by an Israeli, on behalf of her people, for all violence and transgressions perpetrated by Israelis against Palestinians.

In spiritual fellowship, our job is not to make a political stand for either Palestinians or Israelis, but rather to make a spiritual stand for both. Love makes a stand for eternal innocence, not worldly guilt, and we must stand on that love like a rock. On the Sabbath we articulate an alternative vision for life on Earth, that humanity might grow into it. In holding to our conviction that all souls are innocent, we're helping to create the space in which that innocence will shine forth.

The next evening, I participated in a peace circle along with several people who had been present at the Sabbath service the day before. One woman who had not been to that

Sabbath service began to express her upset over the violence in the Middle East. As she spoke, it was obvious that she blamed one side more than the other, and as such her mind was still at the level of the problem, not the Answer. For the presumption of spiritual innocence is the only real answer. Those at whom we point fingers never represent our biggest problem: Our biggest problem is that we point fingers at all. For those of us who had been at the Sabbath service and experienced the spiritual power of the apologies, guilt didn't overwhelm our perceptions. Our minds were oriented differently, not taking sides in the battle, but lifted by God above the battlefield. And I realized again why the Sabbath is so important, why it is so essential to gather together and ask, "How would God view this?" Then for the rest of the week we can be conduits of a wisdom that we could only have received through His illumination. We observe the Sabbath not in order to give up worldly things, but in order to give up a worldly perspective.

Notice that the commandment reads, "Observe the Sabbath." In order to receive the blessing of the Sabbath, we must observe it. It's like the difference between knowing that the Super Bowl is on television today and actually sitting down to watch it; the idea and the experience are two different things. Bringing idea and experience together on the Sabbath, we recommit to our inner covenant with a living

God. Then we are repaired and reenergized for the days ahead.

Yet how are we to celebrate the Sabbath if we don't feel tied to a particular religion? The realization of spiritual realities supersedes doctrinal direction, and the Sabbath is a concept that transcends religion. We can make our own Sabbath service with friends at home, lighting candles and saying prayers, reading aloud from sacred texts, sharing a meal in fellowship and communion. Observation of the Sabbath is a movement within the heart, more than an external attendance at a religious service. Some people might feel a desire to observe the Sabbath in solitude, allowing the day to be one of communion with God separate from fellowship or the experience of community. God is everywhere and He is in everything: Sabbath is important as the day we spend with Him, whatever that looks like and however it suits the individual. Modern mysticism doesn't seek to dictate worldly form but to emphasize spiritual content.

Like everything else, life is as deep or as shallow as we wish to play it. A holy Sabbath is in the depths of the spiritual sea, where the soul swims as deep as we are ready to swim, as far as we are prepared to go, and as close to God as we dare to be. As we swim toward Him, we realize He swims toward us. In awe and in rapture, at last we become the sea.

# Holidays

Holidays have become desanctified in America today. The fire wall separating the concerns of commerce from the concerns of God now seems to have crumbled, as we render unto Caesar what is Caesar's, and frequently render unto him what is God's as well.

Many of us know this and don't like it, yet the cultural undertow has been tugging at us for years. Like swimmers along the shore, we could have sworn we were far down the beach just a little while ago. We have no idea how we got where we are, having been pulled along by a force much more powerful than ourselves. Slowly and insidiously, the values of the marketplace have begun to dominate our entire culture.

Presidents' Day has become less a day to deeply honor great souls, such as Abraham Lincoln, and their contributions to the history of our nation than a day to take advantage of the Presidents' Day sales at malls across America. Memorial Day weekend has become less a day to deeply honor those who have died for our country than a weekend for barbecues, travel, and visiting friends. Christmas has become so commercialized that the miraculous birth of Jesus gets practically swallowed up by the materialism surrounding it. And Martin Luther King, Jr.'s birthday? Great! The kids can get a day off school!

Days of honor thus become days of dishonor, as ego concerns take center stage time and time again and the spirit of love, the spirit of God, is pushed aside. But those of us who wish for a deeper experience of the holidays should remember that we are responsible for our own thinking. We can embrace the deeper meaning of the holidays that matter to us, celebrating the days on which they occur from a place of serious wonder and awe. We don't need to go along with the pack; indeed, we can consciously repudiate the shallower thought forms that pervade it. Sometimes you can feel there's an undertow, but choose to try to swim across it with every bit of strength that you have.

Every year, weeks before Christmas and Hanukkah, I say to people, "Decide right now: Are you going to give this season to God, or are you going to give this season to the ego?" These holidays are about the birth of God and the arrival of miracles. They are about personal transformation and the emergence of a new self. They are not about whose relatives we're going to be with, who we have to buy gifts for, and whether or not we have the money to pay for all of them. Such material considerations rob our energy and eat away at our soul. Yet such anxiety-ridden dynamics will prevail if we surrender to the endless nagging of our ego mind.

In surrendering a situation to God, we are asking Him to give us new thoughts and feelings about it. We are asking His help in deemphasizing things that don't ultimately matter and focusing on what does. We are asking that His thoughts replace our own, that we be lifted by His Spirit to a lighter consciousness and thus a lighter life. The spiritual life is one of mental discipline in which we cleave to higher thought forms because we know they are key to our happiness and peace. Only in Truth do we find a context for life that makes sense of our existence. And only deeper meaning assuages the suffering of the soul. When it comes to the temptation to make Christmas and Hanukkah more about the gifts of the catalogue than the gifts of the spirit, *just say no!*

One rarely hears a Christian say, "I'm not going to Easter

services this year, because I already know what happens." One rarely hears a Jew say, "I'm not going to Passover seder this year, because I already know what happens." True, we know the stories intellectually. Jesus died on the cross, and then he rose. The Jews were in bondage, then Moses led them to the promised land. But religious stories are more than they appear: They are coded messages sent by God, heard by whatever part of our consciousness is open to receive them. If we meet the religious stories with shallow listening, they have shallow effects on our lives. The way we receive God's messages determines in large part what they are. Met superficially, the holidays are superficial. Met with genuine devotion, the holidays are transformative. They are as relevant to our lives as we allow them to be.

Why does the mystic celebrate Christmas? Because the birth of Jesus heralds the opportunity for new life on earth, not just for one man but for the entire human race. Christmas represents the spiritual possibility that we will leave behind who we used to be and become who we were created to be. Mary represents the soul, impregnated by the seed of God, giving birth to the highest possibility within us. We emerge as transformed beings, mothered by our humanity and fathered by God, risen at last to our true reality. The star of Christmas, the light that glowed in a darkened sky, is literally the realization that there lies within us such divine potential. Our mystical union with Mary and Jesus illumines not only our understanding, but also the trajectory of our entire lives. It lifts us into the spiritual vortex of the truth their lives revealed.

Why does the mystic celebrate Hanukkah? Because the oil that the Jews were burning in their lamps was not enough to guarantee their survival, yet the oil continued to burn despite the laws of the physical universe. The Jew is reminded on Hanukkah that the God of our fathers is eternally there for us, aware of our suffering and committed to its end. He is the flame that casts out all darkness. For it is the light of God, not the light of the world, that nourishes and sustains us. To know this and remember it is to keep our living covenant with Him.

And why does the mystic celebrate Easter? Because Jesus' resurrection demonstrated a power that casts out fear, even unto death itself. "Be of good cheer, for I have overcome the world." The message was not that Jesus had *fixed* the world, but rather that he had *overcome* it. He had achieved a perfect love, which then made him invulnerable to the lovelessness of the world. His consciousness had risen so high that in his presence all lower thought forms were rendered null and void. Yes, it would take a symbolic three days, but love prevailed for him and will now prevail for us as well. No matter what has happened, if we should hold on for those "three days"—standing on faith that love and forgiveness will work a miracle for us—then we too will experience a rising up as our hearts and our relationships receive new life. As long as we remain true to love, then love remains true to us. That is the resurrection of Christ.

Why does the mystic celebrate Passover? Because the slavery of the ancient Jews in Egypt is a slavery to which we can all relate. The pharaoh of our ego mind would bind us to the meaninglessness and pain of a life of fear. Yet God lifted up his servant Moses, as He lifts up hope in all of us. All of us feel the whip of Pharaoh, and all of us hear, if we listen well, the voice of Moses calling us out of bondage. Our bondage might be an addiction, a dysfunctional relationship, or a self-defeating pattern. And like the Israelites who initially resisted Moses, we fear the flight to freedom might be worse than our slavery. But, in the words of *A Course in Miracles,* "God will outwit our self-hatred." Finally, the Israelites were delivered, and we will be as well. Though God had to part the waters of the Red Sea to save the Jews from perishing, so He is willing to part the waters for us. In celebrating Passover, we remember that the God of Israel has been there for His people before and will be there always. God's love for us is so immense, we can scarcely recognize the dimensions of its mercy.

To celebrate these holidays is to do much more than buy

presents, open them, cook dinner, show up for dinner, or make children happy. The joy is not just for children. It's for each and every one of us, when we realize the internal dimensions of the great religious holidays. The gift that needs to be unwrapped is the holiday itself. And one need not be Christian to experience the glory of the Christ, or Buddhist to experience the power of the sutras, or Jewish to experience the comfort of God's promises. The mystic responds to universal spiritual themes, all echoing in a different way a unified message from God: The potential of a divinely empowered consciousness lies in every one of us.

From Yom Kippur to Ramadan to solstice celebrations to Christmas to Shivaratri, the great religious holidays—as well as civil holidays celebrating noble civic principles—are ways in which humanity is reminded to keep faith with what is true. We appreciate the miraculous possibilities that the holidays provide: that on Christmas morning, for instance, millions of people consider the possibility of a perfect love; that on Passover, the Jewish people consider the possibility that God is here to deliver us even now; that on Easter morning, millions of people consider the possibility that through love we can transcend all limitations of the world—such is the power of the religious holidays, when we consider their invisible influence on hearts throughout the world.

And how do we participate in the mystical meaning of

the holidays? Through prayer, quiet, spirit-filled ceremony or fellowship, reading, or any cultivation of deeper meaning that works for us. We might fast, meditate, sing, or build altars in our homes; we might read spiritual books with our families or create new rituals that deepen our experience of ageless truths. And, most important, we pray. For prayer, in the words of *A Course in Miracles,* is the "conduit of miracles." We need simply pray that God reveal to us, in our own life, the meaning of a holiday. And watch what happens. He will do the rest.

Once we recognize the real power of holidays, we begin to approach them with deeper devotion. A holiday is a holy day, and holiness doesn't happen to us. Holiness is a choice we make, and holidays are portals of energy through which the experience of things that matter most is increased within us and in the world in which we live. Bear witness to what happened to someone else two thousand years ago or more, and you will enter the timeless dimension in which it is happening to you.

# Relationships

French philosopher Jean Paul Sartre wrote that "hell is other people." People are heaven, too, of course, when relationships go well and people behave the way we wish. Either way, people are hard to get away from in this world, and our relationships with others go far toward determining our happiness or lack of it.

I remember that when my daughter was a baby, I kept wishing she could talk because I wanted to have a conversation with her. And now that she's talking as fast and as much as her mother, I remember how sweet it was when no matter what I said, she just looked up at me adoringly, giggling, never arguing! So if I want sweet and cuddly relationships with no disagreements, I might want to hang around infants. But if I want intelligent dialogue, I'd better get out my magic wands. People over the age of three have a way of saying what they actually think, which may or may not make your day.

The character of our relationships ranges from the heights of enlightenment to the depths of destruction, and most of us have been privy to both at some point in our lives. As with any other situation, the key to making and keeping relationships harmonious lies in placing them in the hands of God.

To place a situation in the hands of God, as we know, is to place our *thinking* in the hands of God. It means we're asking His Spirit to enter our minds and guide our perceptions. We're asking Him to help us remain focused on the divine essence in someone else and help them remain focused on the divine essence in us. We are asking that the possibilities of the present, not the mistakes of the past, guide our perceptions of each other and ourselves.

The key to right relationship—and every situation is, in some way, a relationship—is to allow each one, in every moment, to be lifted from the past. A relationship is reborn whenever we see someone as they are right now and don't hold them to who they were. Focus on the present, not the past, is essential to the experience of grace.

Relationships represent assignments made by Divine Intelligence, bringing together those who represent the greatest opportunities for learning from each other. In every relationship, there's an endless stream of potential healing, both for the people joined in the original encounter and for countless others they will each meet in turn. In *A Course in Miracles,* they are referred to as "laboratories of the Holy Spirit." Every relationship is a temple of God, blessed by love and innocence or desecrated by fear and guilt. Which it is, is up to us.

The mystic is always guarding his or her thoughts, seeking to drop the thoughts that condemn and extend the thoughts that bless. For there is no such thing as a thought that goes unnoticed by the universe. This is both exciting and horrifying when we think about it. For we can all be so judgmental at times, *even toward those we truly love.*

Yet our emotional reality is ultimately our own responsibility. We can *decide* to bless someone, even if we don't like his or her behavior, and in doing so we're freed from the limited vision by which we judged him or her to begin with. It's our willingness to see the innocence in someone, even when they have shown us their guilt, that gives us the capacity to transform both their experience and our own.

While we are born with a perfect capacity to love, each of us is tempted by the realities of life to withhold our love and defend against pain. Compassion, defenselessness, and unconditional love are much easier to express before we become aware of how dangerous life and love can be. Only very small children—and saints—are really very good at it.

Yet our alternative to reaching for the angels is to slide down the slippery slope to hell. Hell is not a place we go after we die. Hell is right here on earth, and all of us have visited it at one time or another. It's the suffering of separation from those with whom we are already joined as one. Separation from others is a separation from God, and nothing hurts more, nor drives us more insane.

There is something to learn from every encounter. If someone is kind to us, the lesson is to be grateful, not to take kindness for granted, and, most important, to graciously return their kindness. If someone is not kind, the lesson is to rise above that, because reacting to them is like throwing gasoline on a fire. Anger does nothing more than deplete our personal power. As Jacqueline Kennedy Onassis once said to a friend, "Only amateurs stay mad."

Someone who behaves in a non-loving way has simply forgotten who they are, and the role of the miracle worker is to remind them of the truth by remaining in touch with it ourselves. Our job is to remain awake to the eternal innocence at the heart of everyone, that in our presence other people might wake up to it as well. The light in our own mind will help dissolve the darkness in someone else's, but only if we refuse to judge or blame them for what we view as their errors. Our perception of someone's essential innocence as a child of God *is* the light, in a metaphysical sense, while our focus on someone's guilt *is* the darkness. To cast "light" on something simply means to understand it more deeply.

If we are in serious conflict with someone, there are often limits to how much can actually be achieved by personal communication. On the level of personality, the walls that divide us can be too thick to tear down through mortal means alone. Phone calls, letter writing, or conversation are not always measures that would be received well.

Sometimes we say we have communicated with someone, when all we really did was share our own viewpoint. The word "communication" has the same root as the word "communion," and where there is no communion there is no true communication. Only when we have taken responsibility for the heartspace between ourselves and another, practicing humility and forgiveness as best we can, can we say true communication has occurred.

When the walls that divide us seem impenetrable, we can repair to our inner room, our holy sanctuary, to spiritually work out our differences with others. When we dedicate our relationship to God at its genesis, we are ministered to by angels as we progress within the relationship. And whether we have dedicated it or not, the key to healing relationships is to go back to God, asking for a miraculous shift in perception from guilt and fear to innocence and love. Sometimes both parties are willing to join in prayer and ask for this, and sometimes only one is willing. Yet one is enough. According to *A Course in Miracles,* "whoever is saner at the time" can call on the Holy Spirit to enter a relationship. And no prayer goes unheard.

In the inner room, there *are* no differences between or among us. Whether an argument between friends or a war between nations, God does not choose sides. Rather, He removes the walls that divide us. Those walls primarily live in our minds, and it is God's love reaching beyond the level of human drama that has the power to dissolve them. It finds a way to remind us who we are. It delivers us from the drama of "who did what to whom" and to the truth of our innocence *regardless* of who did what to whom. By looking to the sky instead of to the earth for answers, we spread our wings and fly above trials and tribulations that otherwise would keep us down. For it is only in looking beyond a problem that we have the power to resolve it. Everyone makes mistakes; we all have bad days, get in rotten moods, and say or do things we wish we hadn't. We would be much better off—and certainly our relationships would improve—were we to take every moment's word and deed less seriously and to trust in the deeper intentions of the heart.

I once heard something nasty someone said about me, and I shared my distress with a mutual friend. He said to me, "Well, she might have said it, but that doesn't change the fact that I know she loves you." When he said that, I remembered that I have made flip judgmental comments about people I love, and how horrified I would have been had they heard. It didn't really matter if my friend had said something unkind about me; it was up to me whether to attach meaning to it or release it as not important. On the spiritual mountaintop, we are kind to one another all the time. But in the meantime, we can stop taking it so seriously when we are not.

Even if someone doesn't like you, they love you whether they know it or not. And it's worth telling them that in meditation. "I know you dislike me, but I refuse to dislike you. I hold to the Truth of our connection as God created it, I hold to the Truth of our inner oneness, and I invite the spirit of God to enter here and dissolve the walls between us. I forgive you and I ask that you please forgive me."

Holiness surrounds a relationship with light, so that the

darkness of blame and judgment has less chance of clouding our thoughts to begin with. That's why the beginning of a relationship is such a perfect time to surrender it to God, before the ego has a chance to claim it. Beginnings set the tone for what will follow.

> *Dear God,*
> *I place in Your hands*
> *My relationship with ____.*
> *May our relationship serve You.*
> *May we see each other through the eyes of love,*
> *That only Light might enter here.*
> *Thank you, God.*
> *Amen.*

The more mindful and responsible we become, the fewer relationship disasters we will create in our lives. Yet none of us is perfect, and any deep and genuine relationship is bound to arouse temptations to fear instead of love. It's by being forced to recognize the times when we're not yet purely loving, surrendering them into the hands of God, that we grow into the angels we are capable of being.

Prayer will release us from our pain, if we're willing to humble ourselves. Sometimes it is very difficult to admit to ourselves, to God, and particularly to other people that we have been wrong and that we seek forgiveness. Yet it is only when we genuinely come clean with God that He can heal our lives.

While we instinctively understand the power of prayer when there is a problem, we tend to underestimate its power when there is not. We don't usually stop to say a prayer *before* the meeting, or *before* the date, or *before* the relationship gets going. We think, *Why should I say a prayer now? There's no problem!* But the sly and insidious ego is always on the alert for ways to separate the children of God, just as God is always on the alert for ways to reconnect our hearts. Prayer has a way of rendering the ego powerless, reminding the mind of our eternal innocence. And therein lies our salvation.

Relationships are where the ego seeks to do battle with the will of God. In reality, there *is* no battle, for those whom God hath joined together—and he has joined all of us to all of us—cannot be put asunder. It is only our thinking that we are separate from others that dooms us to conflict and struggle and pain.

Often, when someone criticizes us, the pain of their judgment makes it difficult for us to realize that some aspect of what they are saying might be correct. While the message may be delivered in words that seem unfair, there is often still a message worth hearing. The more spiritually mature mind burns through the pain of hearing important information from someone whom we would rather not hear from at all, asking, "Is there some personality trait I've been carrying around for years that is possibly contributing to someone's dislike? Is it something I might surrender and transform?"

The work of the mystic is not so much to make ourselves better as to be honest about who we are right now. When we are candid with ourselves and with God, then we can release to Him the issues that we know need healing, and thus be purified by His spirit. Our best intentions to "act better" don't mean all that much; our willingness to have Him *make* us better means everything.

It is not always our own darkness—indeed, sometimes it's the very fact that we have shone our light—that attracts other people's judgment. But then a profound lesson lies in realizing how threatening our own light can be. It's important to be conscious of that, lest we subconsciously dim our light in order to avoid offending anyone. We should pray for protection and humility as we shine in our world. For there's no dearth of light on this planet; there's just way too much of it that remains inside us, not shining at all. And *that* is part of the darkness of the world: how afraid we are to shine our own light. In asking God to help us shine, we're asking that His light shine through us.

*Dear God,*
*May Your light burst forth within me,*
*To bathe my inner self*
*and shine through me to bless*
*all living things.*
*Amen.*

We are on the earth to be joyful and to share our joy with others. The spirit looks to relationships as a place to share our happiness, while the ego looks to them to assuage our pain. Our fundamental loneliness, however, lies not in our separation from others but in our separation from self. To say that we are separated from God is not to say that we are separated from something outside ourselves, for God does not lie outside ourselves. It is to say that we are fragmented inside, having experienced a profound split from our own essential nature. We have been lured away by the illusions of the world.

To look for the experience of "home" in anything within the material world is to make the world a trap. For it is not our home. It's a fantastic hotel at best. The realm of physical things—the body included—is the realm of separation, not of true joining. Knowing that, making the focus of our attention the connection of spirits rather than the connection of bodies, gives us a fundamental, spiritual sanity that serves us well in relating to others.

Otherwise, we search the world for something to heal the pain that results from our being too attached to it already. Usually, we will look to *other people* to fix us. We are tempted to enter into relationships on a search for the lost self we cannot find. Yet outside ourselves we cannot find what only lies within. When we look to another to complete us, we doom the relationship because we are subconsciously looking to it to be what it is not. And every time I reach a place in our relationship where I am not in touch with myself, I will behave in a way that repels you. For if I am a yo-yo with myself, I will be a yo-yo with you. That is why healing our inner life is a prerequisite for relating successfully to others.

My family has often joked about the fact that when my mother was pregnant with me, she and my father both felt sure that I was a boy. My father wanted to name me Mordecai. My mother told him in no uncertain terms that I would not be named Mordecai, but it became a joke around the house nonetheless. He said Mordecai, she said Michael; and I have no doubt she would have prevailed, had she given birth to a boy. She did not, of course, yet when my mother brought me home from the hospital, we were greeted at the family apartment with signs all over the place that read, WELCOME HOME, LITTLE MORDECAI!

My mother and I still disagree about this decades later,

but I swear to you I remember those signs. "Great. They wanted somebody else. . . ." And in many ways, as I went through my life, I would re-create that drama in my relationships with others. Feeling in various ways unreceived in my childhood, I desperately sought to be received by others in my later years. But I didn't know how to genuinely accept others into my life, because the pattern had not been modeled for me. So others would end up feeling unreceived by me, and the cycle would repeat itself.

It took a lot more than rational analysis to interrupt that pattern. It could not be broken by finding another person who would finally, ultimately, accept me fully. That could not and would not happen until first I repaired my own underlying wound by learning to accept myself. I learned that I am received by God, and that my job is to help others feel as welcomed by me as we are welcomed by Him. Love is the miracle of a rewired heart, as our relationship with Him redeems our relationships with others.

A man once asked me if I knew any prayers for loneliness. I asked why he was looking for such a prayer; what was wrong in his relationships with others? He said he tried to get close to people but always ended up behaving in a way that was perceived as either needy or haughty. He just wanted a prayer to ease the pain. I understood. But just as we wouldn't pray to simply assuage the pain of a broken leg—we would pray that the leg be healed, as well—I suggested that he pray for God's healing of his neediness and haughtiness first. There was a place in his psyche where his spirit did not feel received, and so it went to sleep to avoid the pain. There, in that place, the hand of God, not the hand of man, has the capacity to heal us.

God does not wish for us to be lonely, and, in the fullness of ourselves, we are not. But God is not found outside our relationship with the rest of life—He *is* our relationship with the rest of life. When our desire to relate to life is a desire to share our joy, extending beyond thoughts that would separate us to thoughts that would bless and unite us with others, then loneliness fades. The key is not to build relationships; the key is to give up the many concepts that shroud us from this awesome fact: We are related already. We are one in spirit—how much more related can we be?

With every human encounter, God gives us the chance to re-create our world. We can extend beyond the boundaries of our isolated existence and bless the person, salute the angel, open our hearts to the similarly wounded one who stands before us. Or we can refuse to do those things, feeling the pain of having someone else withhold from us their blessing, their salute, their love. There is nothing and no one outside us, so much as there are mirrors everywhere. Every

person is a part of us, and we are a part of every person—
sacred the chalice that holds us together, and painful the
thoughts that would tear us apart. Both are within us. It is
ours to choose.

And we do choose. Constantly.

May we choose the divine.

# Community

It has been said that when the Buddha comes again, he will arrive not as a person but as a community. We will know that God is here on earth when we can see Him in one another.

Once, when I was in my early twenties, I lived in a house in San Francisco with several other people. In the dining room overlooking the city, there was a very long table at which there were always people drinking coffee and engaging in lively conversation at almost any time of the night or day. That was a period of my life in which I thought of my future as more important than my present—surely in my future I would find the secret to happiness. But now that I'm living what my younger self thought of as the future, I look back to that table and think, *That was it!* There at that table, I remember having my first and still one of my most potent experiences of community. My house today is nicer, to be sure. Like others of my generation, I "graduated" into my own this, my own that. But also, like others of my generation, I sort of miss the old days when there was more connection and less competition, more community and less isolation, more conversation and less TV.

Today, when we think about people joining together, it's not always for such wonderful purposes. We know about "terror cells," made up of terrorists joined for the purpose of wreaking havoc on our world. We get chills as we realize the power of two or more terrorists joined together, exerting greater power than the sum of the individuals. Yet the power of joining together applies as much—in fact, much more—to those who love than to those who hate. For there is a cosmic propulsion behind love that is not behind hate. Our problem is not that hate is more powerful than love, because indeed it is not; our problem is that hatred today is more energetic and active than love. It's time for our generation to allow ourselves not only the satisfaction of deep love and community, but also the power of deep love and community. It is the greatest antidote to the darkness of our times.

Metaphysically speaking, God did not create us individually, but as one; that is the esoteric meaning of "only one begotten Son." The awareness of our oneness, while foreign to the ego, is clear to the heart. And that's why unity is the key to our happiness. Spiritually, we do not exist in isolation. It is unnatural for us to perceive ourselves as separate; in fact, we're like sunbeams of the same sun and waves of the same ocean. Imagining ourselves as separate waves, we feel that we are tiny and powerless, when in fact we are integral to the immense power of the sea.

It's only when we transcend the illusion of separation, refusing the false testimony of our physical senses, that we will make the quantum leap forward into a joy-filled life. We will know peace when we learn to love as God loves, and God loves all of us as one. We were created as one and we remain as one. The Golden Rule is so fundamental because what we do to others, we literally are doing to ourselves.

The recognition of our unity is the healing of all our wounds. Yet how do we convert the consciousness of humanity to a perspective of spiritual oneness? And what would the world look like if we did? Every once in a while, we give ourselves a taste of what life on Earth could be like, were we to truly interact like brothers and glimpse a higher possibility for connection among us.

On the final day of the last millennium, as people geared up for New Year's Eve celebrations all over the world, television networks broadcast fireworks displays from London to Sydney, New York to Hong Kong. I remember a particular moment that day, when I was simply walking through my living room, becoming aware of the sense that the entire world was in love. I didn't have the feeling of being in love with a particular person, but of love as a feeling that filled the air, an all-pervasive sweetness such as I had never known. I felt everyone was capable of loving everyone. And in that moment, I thought, *This is how life is supposed to feel. It is how we will feel one day, when we've evolved to our divine potential.* Love did not feel like the exception—it felt like the rule that day. The air itself was peaceful in a way we do not ordinarily experience.

A friend who lives in New York City told me about her remarkable experience on day one of the year 2000, as she was on her way to work. She told me the subway was like one big party. Everyone was celebrating; everyone was kind to each other; people who didn't even know one another were talking and joking. Many of these same people had been riding to work together every day for months or even years, and yet what a difference a day made.

So what really happened on that day? Was there actually an external, objective shift of some sort—or rather, for one shining moment, did we not simply change our social contract? What spell of peace and goodwill came upon us, and why, like Cinderella at the stroke of midnight, did we feel compelled at day's end to go back to who we were before?

Just as Abraham Maslow asserted that studying psychologically well-adjusted people was more revealing, in the end, than studying those who were psychologically impaired, it behooves us to question what is really going on in those moments when we come together in peace. The truth is, nothing objectively occurred on New Year's Day as we entered this millennium. What did occur is that for the period of about one day, we gave ourselves permission to behave like brothers. We reached for a universal love that day, beyond the confines of a particular relationship to an individual or group. Our natural knowing superseded our ego, and we entered into a different, unspoken agreement with one another: This was not to be a day for competition, but for cooperation; not a day for war, but for peace; not a day for judgment, but for blessing; and not a day for unhappiness, but for celebration. Nothing more than a simple shift in how we saw life made the difference that day. It was an internal—not an external—power that tilted us toward the light. We simply changed our perspective.

From that shift in our thinking there arose, if only for a brief time, a different kind of world. For one day, the focus of our attention and genius was on the celebration of life. We saw the world we would want to see, because on that day it was what we *decided* to see. For that one day, we got it right. And if we could do it for a day, then isn't it reasonable to assume that we could do it for longer?

My point is surely idealistic. But what more is an ideal than a thought that has not yet descended from heaven to Earth, a thought that awaits the evolution of the human race to be accepted and made manifest? Wasn't the abolition of slavery once merely an ideal? Wasn't women's suffrage once merely an ideal? Wasn't the end of Britain's colonial rule in India once merely an ideal? Idealism, after all, is not a *neurosis*. What is neurotic is how little idealism we display anymore, how lacking in imagination we've become about anything beyond individual goals. Now is the time for collective goals and collective ideals, as our near-fanatical adherence to the belief in separation has reached such dangerous proportions. Realism is not particularly helpful when what is real is so painful to witness. What is idealism, after all, but a message from the Real to the real? It's the force that inspires us to improve the world with a deep inner knowing that something better is possible. An ideal is a pure idea that becomes miraculous when blended with human imagination and effort. Great ideas need not languish in the realm of abstract possibility; they are meant to be embodied. Through the willingness of people and the grace of God, they become part of our earthly experience whenever we choose.

Another example of a heightened state of group awareness occurs every two years at the Olympic games. While charges of corruption have soiled their reputation at times, the basic sensibility of the Olympics is one of enlightened, joy-filled competition. The unique talents and brilliance of all nations are on display in a stunning demonstration of human community. As the athletes march in for the opening ceremonies, our hearts thrill at the reminder of how things could be. We see nations of the world recognizing each other as fellow citizens of the planet, all created with special talents, expressing themselves fully and delighting in one another's magnificence. We get a glimpse of what's possible, and we can feel that the Olympic Torch symbolizes something much more than sportsmanship. There's a universal sanctity to its flame, as it clearly represents a light that shines in every person and every heart, calling us to wholeness of body, mind, and spirit.

Comparing the Olympics to the state of our world today, we are tempted to despair. It is hard to accept the simultaneous reality of such noble genius as Olympian athleticism and terrorist destruction. Yet both exist, and both are real within our experience. They arise from very different views of our purpose on this Earth, and one—not both—will ultimately prevail.

It's important for the spiritual activist to remember that things could be different in our world, that the moments we experience as magnificent exceptions could indeed become the rule. Robert F. Kennedy often quoted George Bernard Shaw in saying, "Some people see things as they are and ask, 'Why?' I think of how they could be, and I ask, 'Why not?' "

Children holding flowers could greet us when we arrive in a new country, instead of customs agents and guards. People could live in abundance and peace, instead of poverty and war. Life could be a continuous dance of harmony for everyone, instead of a desperate struggle to survive for so many. Once we are ready to accept such a vision and consider it possible, because in God all things are possible, then our lives will become channels through which it will emerge. It's only a failure of imagination that keeps us stuck in patterns of limitation and fear.

There is a new peace movement emerging today among those who realize that our spiritual powers afford us tremendous opportunity to transform the world. We can imagine the world we want, we can become the people from whom that world would flow forth, and we can join with others in making it happen. There are millions among us who understand we are one. As we create deeper peace among any of us anywhere, the reality of peace becomes more probable everywhere. We can surround the world with a field of peace so powerful that hatred and fear will dissolve in its presence.

Scientists tell us we live in a holographic universe, which means that, on the level of energy, the whole is contained in every piece and every piece contains the whole. So it is that a healing between or among any of us literally helps to heal all of us. Any time walls that divide us melt, the world is brought closer to the reuniting of hearts, which is the mystical goal of human existence.

Peace is more than the absence of war; it's the presence of peace, a positive state of being that is predicated on brotherhood and justice and love. In its presence, injustice and hatred have little power to grow. That is why knowing the truth of our spiritual oneness and embracing it within our hearts is the ultimate answer to all the problems of the world. At the level of spiritual reality, none of us are separate. The body has differences; the spirit does not. Community arising from the realization of our oneness is community that goes beyond mere alliance or treaty. It stems from a knowing of the heart, which transforms the mind. Emerging from our depth, it touches others in the same place. And thus what was broken apart shall be mended.

The horrors of the world we live in today arise from spiritual ignorance. Until we reach that place in ourselves where we identify with one another beyond our differences, we will perpetuate the disharmony that results from spiritual immaturity. Technological and material progress, alas, is not necessarily accompanied by spiritual wisdom. Often, in fact, our material power is used by the ego as a way to resist the Truth. Yet the Truth remains and catches up with us in time: There's no material shield that our karma will not penetrate.

We cannot escape one another, and in our right minds we wouldn't want to. Spending extraordinary resources trying to protect ourselves from our fellow human beings, rather than on efforts to build righteous relationships, is a backward model of human interaction. And the fact that we don't quite know how to turn our civilization from a war machine into a peace machine is not a reason not to try. Perhaps all the problems on the earth today provide us an opportunity, a challenge to surrender to the Truth in our hearts. Perhaps the mortal mind has been pushed at last into the proverbial corner, where we'll admit to our inability to save ourselves—indeed, to our genius at destroying ourselves—and humbly ask God to do for us what we cannot do for ourselves. Man is very effective at waging war; God is most effective at waging peace.

Jesus told us to love our enemies and bless those who curse us. To pray for someone is to pray that they be returned to their right minds. What a thought, given the state of the world today. If every one of us took one minute a day to close our eyes and send the love of God to Al Qaeda, we would have far, far less to worry about. In your mind, surround any violent person with a diamond egg: No malevolence will be able to penetrate the hardness of the diamond, while its light will shine back on their hearts and heal their minds. With this mystical remedy, they are spiritually quarantined.

We will be brothers and sisters in peace—and not war—when that is what we decide to call forth. Until then, we will face the consequences of our not yet having chosen love as the organizing principle for human civilization. Building genuine connection and deep community among the peoples of the world is the historical task of our generation. Where our governments do not seem equal to that task— indeed, in some cases they clearly repudiate it—we ourselves must strive to accomplish it nevertheless. With love in our hearts, we can supersede all fear-based consciousness, no matter how much material power it might wield. We will forge a new field of human possibility in which war shall be no more.

In the meantime, we will continue to gravitate to long

dining-room tables where friends await us; we will continue to fall in love on blessed, enchanted days; and we will continue to fervently love our children and watch their miraculous dance into adulthood. But there will be more. Now, in an extraordinary moment of global transformation, we will do more than just love: We will join our love and harness our love. We will pool our resources of forgiveness and imagination and grace, and in time we will collectively experience what physicists call "phase lock," a phenomenon in which individual oscillating rhythms—here, the beats of many, many hearts around the world—fall into a deep pattern of energetic resonance. We will form a community of consciousness—a collective love—that is humanity's next step on our evolutionary journey. Love is not meant to be alone. It reaches out to find itself at every opportunity.

Scientists tell us about "phase lock"—not that it always happens, but that it is always *trying* to happen. No matter how much havoc fear and hatred wreak, God has a better plan that is incapable of failure. It lacks not power but adherents. It waits simply for us to say "yes" to love as energetically as hatred says "no." Thus shall be the deliverance of the world, when we arise from our stupor and faithlessness and doubt, and create the world we were born to create. First we will do this in tiny increments, and at last in waves of huge significance. An awe-filled grace will fill the skies and flood our hearts, when we have remembered at last who we are to one another.

That we *are* one another.

Praise God.

Amen.